FOR
OUTDOOR MENTORS,

NAMED AND UNNAMED
PAST, PRESENT AND FUTURE

AND FOR
LYDIAN AND REED

BY FORREST ALTMAN ❖ DRAWINGS BY STACEY HELLER
COVER DESIGN BY ELIZABETH N. ALTMAN ❖ MAPS BY JOHN CLEAVELAND
LAYOUT BY RENÉE WESTERFIELD ❖ STAR SQUARE PRESS

"26 Wilderness Adventures: Afoot and Afloat."
Text ©1999 by Walter Forrest Altman. Illustrations ©1999 by Stacey Shumate Heller. All rights reserved. Printed in the United States of America. No part of this book may be used or reproduced in any manner without written permission except in the case of brief quotations embodied in critical articles and reviews. For information, address Star Square Press, 1200 Jack Pointer Road, Semora NC 27343-9437;
Telephone +1-336-234-8556.

First Edition, 1999

Versions of the following first appeared in the *Caswell Messenger*: "The Antaeus Effect," "High Point on Bigwater Lake." "The Dan at Flood," "Suggestions for a Rainy Day" and "Okefenokee with Sammy Oliver."

A version of "Following the Holy Cross" and portions of "Bittersweet Mistletoe Report" first appeared in *The Paddler*, newsletter of the Carolina Canoe Club.

Other bits have appeared in *The Source*, newsletter of the Headwaters Group of the Sierra Club, Durham, North Carolina.

Library of Congress Catalogue Number 99-96636

Altman, Walter Forrest
    26 Wilderness Adventures: Afoot and Afloat. Illustrated by Stacey Shumate Heller. First Edition

ISBN 0-9652081-2-5

Printed in the United States of America by
MORRIS PUBLISHING
3212 East Highway 30 • Kearney, Nebraska 68847 • 800-650-7888

26 Wilderness Adventures Afoot & Afloat

By Forrest Altman

FOREWORD

THE TALES WE TELL

The marriage of storytelling and wilderness wandering is a natural combination and a social institution. Outdoor people — hikers and hunters, paddlers and anglers, campers of all types — have time honored campfire and "cracker barrel" traditions. For many of us, much of the pleasure of being in the boondocks is in sharing the stories as we go. It creates camaraderie, a bond with each other and the places we love. We enjoy bouncing our experiences and observations off each other, entertaining and teaching and learning from each other, and perhaps most importantly, gaining valued and worthwhile memories — a measure of our lives.

The book before you holds some of the shared stories and collected memories of an often wise and always colorful individual, a student and lover of nature and a lifelong traveler of trails: Forrest Altman. The sun-grizzled wilderness storyteller is an archetype and a literary cliché, and like most clichés, it is an expression of truth. Personally, I aspire to be that character. Some of my younger cohorts assure me I'm already there. I'm flattered, mostly. At any rate, at this point in his life's adventure, it is fair to say that Forrest Altman is most assuredly there. He embraces the role and he plays it well. This is his journal and a testament to the life outdoors.

If you are fortunate, if you travel the wild places afoot and afloat as Forrest has done, you can mark your life by your adventures. My wife, Joy, has the words ". . . life between swamp trips . . ." programmed on her computer's screen saver, a reminder that the meetings and management are interludes rather than the whole of her existence. She marks her life — and ours — by the time we spend in the Okefenokee and on our land on Big Creek just north of the swamp. Many of Joy's stories are tales of discovery: remote and largely forgotten water trails found and paddled, the walk on the moon-limned trail that inspired an epiphany, the powerful realization that most people have no idea how bright the full moon really is. But most of her stories punctuate periods in her life, serving as the mileposts of memory: a fishing trip off Belmar with her dad. Rowing across Lake

George with her brother. Building boardwalks in Cheesequake State Park. And later, with me, fishing in the Neuse below Raleigh's Old Milburnie Dam, her first trip through the River Narrows, a long cold swim in the Nantahala. Dragging a canoe over logs in the South River in the dark of a cold October night. Her first trip on the crystal waters of a Florida spring run. Solo canoeing on the black waters of the Waccamaw, the stream's edge bushes hung thick with snakes. Swimming with salamanders in the pools of Pisgah's Steele Creek. The night herons and swallowtail kites of the Wambaw Creek Wilderness and a raucous roost of egrets, herons and ibises on one of the mangrove-studded Ten Thousand Islands. A canoe trip on Turner River and wood storks feeding along the L-28 Canal. Kayaking to Bear Island. Watching the sunset and moonrise over the High Sierra and the full moon illuminating the vast silences of the Boundary Waters. Forrest has dated the trip reports in this anthology, and I suspect they mark a keen sense of the passage of time. Like my wife, he's prone to muse upon the existential irony that change is the Universe's only constant.

All of us whose lives move to the natural rhythms, who feel that compelling link to wild places, have tales to tell. If we were very, very fortunate, these stories span the generations. One of my grandmothers, Elba Wilson, is an accomplished teller of tales. She has held me spellbound with the story of the "painter"* that stalked and flanked her father along a dark north Georgia mountain road, saddened me with her observations of the last great chestnuts dying, angered me with her accounts of the loggers who "peeled those mountains like peeling an orange," awed me with the knowledge that my "Paw Paw," Frank Wilson, fed his depression-era family on wild hogs he live-trapped in the Smokies. In keeping with her tradition, I hope to pass my own tales of woods and water on to my nieces and nephews and the other children in my life. My own stories of camping in the Black Forest and the Bavarian Alps with my family when my dad was stationed in Germany and of playing Huckleberry Finn in the woods around Lake Lanier when he was in Vietnam. Of a bitterly cold canoe trip on Missouri's Big Piney River and a snow-covered camp at Meramac Caverns when Dad came home again. Of night wanderings in the Blue Ridge foothills as a Boy Scout and canoe trips on Mitchell River. My adulthood has been one long saga of joyous explorations and of painful lessons salved by the balms of wilderness and good friends. Seeking the solace of the Suwannee after a bad business deal. An Okefenokee honeymoon with Joy. A canoe trip with David, a friend now departed, when both the fish and the bugs were biting. River floats and offshore

* panther

fishing with Randy, paddling the Ocala with Bob and Donna and Elmer and other nice people whose names I've forgotten. Canoe trips with Scott and Carol and Tim and Rachel and Joe and Pam. Exploring Garner Creek and Devil's Gut and Sweetwater Creek with Joe and building a camping platform in Upper Deadwater Slough with the Roanoke River Partners. Paddling a 35-mile day on the Black and Cape Fear Rivers and a 16.5-mile day with Don. Three days on Great Dismal Swamp's Lake Drummond with my yellow Lab, Crockett. Dozens of Merchant's Millpond trips and the trips they have inspired: to Bennett's Millpond, Blake's Reserve, Rhodes Pond and Bank's Lake. Scores of Okefenokee excursions, my wilderness homeland, and numerous explorations of some part of every major freshwater wetland and river swamp system between New Jersey's Great Swamp and Florida's Everglades, almost all of them with Joy, my cuddly, cute and constant life's companion. I love the way the place names flow across my lips, like poetry or songs.

And because it has been said that it isn't true wilderness unless there's something out there that can eat you, I love telling the tales of the hunters, of "nature red in tooth and claw": the stories about watching a black bear's nostrls flare as he tried to locate me (I was sitting very, very still in a canoe right out in front of him, about bumping into a bobcat, about two young bears and a camera out of reach, about the howls of the red wolves in the pocosins, about alligators galore — big gators, baby gators, bellowing gators, a few belligerent gators, the startled gator that nearly landed in my lap, even "gator surfing," which is what happens when you surprise an alligator in water shallower than the reptile is deep and it blasts under your boat like a torpedo in its haste to get away, lifting you up and spinning you around and tightening your sphincter tremendously.

So many stories . . .

I had read Forrest's lyrical journal of the Dan River and heard of his Sierra Club work, but I did not actually meet him until recently, when we paddled the ancient bald cypress forests of North Carolina's Black River together with Bob Underwood and Doug Foote. Forrest is a great talker — it takes one to know one — so we got along famously, regaling each other with swamp yarns and river tales and the exploits of our aged dogs. Forrest even had his long-time canine companion, Rusty the Ready River Dog, inscribe a copy of his autobiography to my old buddy, Crockett. A few weeks later, Forrest attended my Pro Canoe presentation on canoeing the Okefenokee Swamp, a place you'll travel in these pages. I was honored when he asked me to review the manuscript of this book.

Reading his tales was like being back on the Black River. It was the same fellow: equal parts Renaissance man and raconteur, at once thoughtful and brash, a sincere and devoted advocate of conservation and of a life defined by explorations of woods and water trails. Bright and bawdy, sometimes subtle but usually not, he is humble enough to include accounts of his misadventures, including lost trails, upset canoes and personality clashes. That speaks to his honesty — it's easy to portray yourself as the all-knowing sage when you're writing your own stories. The words of this volume are his true voice. It's the voice of someone you'll enjoy getting to know.

Forrest Altman loves telling his stories. His joy in the journeys, even the difficult ones, is obvious, as is his passion for the wild and natural. Some of the accounts are rich with vivid descriptions, even incidental plot; most are anecdotes and simple observations. They are the straightforward chronicles of one person's relationship with the natural pathways and connections, with his fellow travelers and with the wilderness within — honest writing, the kind that reveals more about the author than the author even realizes. Like other writers, poets, philosophers, Forrest tries to convey and define the awakened atavistic sense, the reordering of the jangled psyche, the profound personal and spiritual implications of water and wind and woods, of stars and sunsets and snakes. But mostly he just tells his wilderness tales.

Enjoy your time with Forrest Altman. Let him take you on some great outings. Then go out and let your own feet and paddles write stories of their own.

Be careful and have fun.

Chip Campbell
Stem, North Carolina
August 20, 1999

CONTENTS

Foreword: **THE TALES WE TELL** *by Chip Campbell*   **VI**
Introduction: **THE ANTAEUS EFFECT**: *a Testimonial*   **XII**

Part One: **LEGS STRIDING, ARMS SWINGING: 13 TRIPS AFOOT**

ONE - AFOOT   Toes for Seeing   **4**
West Chester, Pennsylvania, 1945

TWO - AFOOT   Mancos Cañon Side-Winder   **10**
Mesa Verde National Park, Colorado, 1950

THREE - AFOOT   Bear-ly Asleep   **18**
Great Smoky Mountains National Park, North Carolina, 1963

FOUR - AFOOT   Traffic Cop in Linville Gorge   **22**
Pisgah National Forest, North Carolina, 1965

FIVE- AFOOT   True-Life Adventure Atop Mt. Sterling   **26**
Great Smoky Mountains National Park, North Carolina, 1967

SIX - AFOOT   Brown Bears and Blueberries   **30**
Appalachian Trail near Clingman's Dome, Tennessee, 1968

SEVEN - AFOOT   Mitchell Falls Initiation   **36**
Mt. Mtchell State Park, North Carolina, 1973

EIGHT - AFOOT   Idyll on Bull Island   **46**
Cape Romain National Wildlife Refuge, South Carolina, 1975

NINE - AFOOT   Comin' 'Round Mt. Rogers   **52**
Mt. Rogers National Recreation Area, Virginia, 1978

TEN - AFOOT   Harper by Moonlight   **58**
Harper Creek Wilderness, North Carolina, 1982

ELEVEN - AFOOT   Summer / Winter with an Outdoor Guru   **66**
Doughton Park, Blue Ridge Parkway / Uwharrie National Forest, North Carolina, 1989

TWELVE - AFOOT   Listening to Chris   **78**
Merchants Millpond State Park, North Carolina, 1989

THIRTEEN - AFOOT   Climbing Ktaadn   **86**
Baxter State Park, Maine, 1991

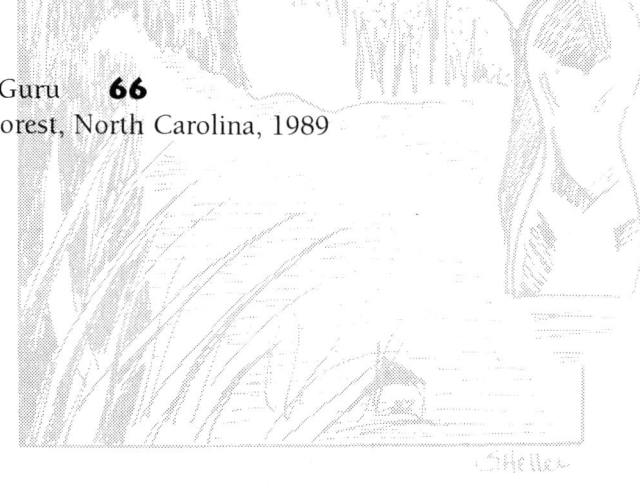

Part Two: **ARMS PULLING, BACK BENDING: 13 TRIPS AFLOAT**

ONE - AFLOAT   Green on the New   **96**
New River, Ashe County, North Carolina, 1976

TWO - AFLOAT   New on the Green   **102**
Green River, Polk County, North Carolina, 1976

THREE - AFLOAT   Lumbee River Serendipity   **108**
Lumbee River, Scotland / Hoke Counties, North Carolina, 1976

FOUR - AFLOAT   Sprig Outing in Little River Swamp   **114**
Harnett County, near Lillington, North Carolina, 1982

FIVE - AFLOAT   Searching for the Giant Cypress   **120**
Merchants Millpond State Park, Gates County, North Carolina, 1980s

SIX - AFLOAT   Okefenokee I: High Point on Bigwater Lake   **126**
Okefenokee National Wildlife Refuge, Georgia / Florida, 1979

SEVEN - AFLOAT   Facing Wind and Tide   **134**
Bear Island, / Intracoastal Waterway, / Hammocks Beach State Park, North Carolina, 1983

EIGHT - AFLOAT   Dualities Down East   **146**
Green Swamp / Waccamaw River, Columbus County, North Carolina

NINE - AFLOAT   The Dan at Flood   **154**
Dan River, Stokes County, North Carolina, 1987

TEN - AFLOAT   Following the Holy Cross   **162**
St. Croix River, Maine / New Brunswick Border, 1991

ELEVEN - AFLOAT   Suggestions for a Rainy Day   **170**
Flat River, Durham County, North Carolina, 1991

TWELVE - AFLOAT   Okefenokee II with Sammy Oliver   **176**
Okefenokee National Wildlife Refuge, Georgia / Florida, 1988

THIRTEEN - AFLOAT   Bittersweet Mistletoe Report   **188**
Little / Lumbee Rivers, North Carolina, 1980s, 1990s

THE MYTHOLOGY OF MISTLETOE (Sir James Frazer)   **199**

GLOSSARY   **201**

ACKNOWLEDGMENTS   **204**

AFTERWORD by Dennis Chorley   **205**

BY WAY OF INTRODUCTION —

THE ANTAEUS EFFECT
A Testimonial

According to Greek mythology, Antaeus was a Libyan king, a giant and a powerful wrestler. In his matches he wore down his opponents because each time he was pressed to Earth he received great power. Legend says that Hercules defeated him by holding him high in the air, out of touch with Earth.

Like most other stories preserved from Greek antiquity, this one contains powerful teaching — if our ears are open. I'll illustrate.

In the 1970s I lived in Charlotte, North Carolina. I liked the city for its political and social climate and its cultural opportunities, but something was missing. I was being swallowed by the city; I needed to be in touch with Earth.

I lived in an apartment. My bedroom was on the second floor, too far from Earth. I worked in the concrete city surrounded by too few trees. I went to meetings in air-conditioned rooms that muffled the sound of birdsong.

One Sunday, driving in the city, I rescued a damsel in distress, a young lady out riding on a bicycle, the tires of which needed air almost as much as I did. Unfortunately, most service stations were closed. I had something which she needed: transportation for her and the bike. In turn, she gave me something of immense and lasting value: information about the Sierra Club, of which she was the local program chair.

Life for me hasn't been the same since. I've had all the outdoor opportunities I require — first to be led into the wilderness by experienced outdoor persons — and then to lead outings myself.

Each experience in the wilderness has taught me — and will teach anyone who ventures forth — something about survival and renewal through connectedness with Nature.

Many persons today are disconnected — or perhaps have never been connected at all. They rarely go outside. They depend on air conditioning for comfort, television for entertainment, the restaurant and the supermarket for all of their food and the mall for clothing and diversion. Cutting the grass may be their only contact with the growing world.

Even in a small town, the sound of traffic is never absent, and one person's music is another person's noise pollution. In the country we are "entertained" by high-flying jets and low-flying military helicopters. Still, it's easier in the country to be close to Earth. If my neighbors are noisier than I might prefer in the daytime, evening brings quiet and wood-thrush music, fireflies and katydids, the moon and the Pleiades and, toward midnight, the barred owl and the whip-poor-will.

Nature can heal, challenge, threaten, sustain, inform, inspire. I pity those who do not know her.

What can we do for them?

Take them outside.

Let them breathe real air, and feel the wind and the sun; study the stars, track the phases of the moon (and sense the moon's power, as the ocean tides do).

Let them learn local plants and animals and grow taller for their walks with the trees.

Let them learn Nature's power by running rapids or sailing before the wind.

Let them learn Nature's fickleness by planting a garden.

So long as Earth is left us, the Antaeus effect is within our reach.

Forrest Altman
Star Square, 1999

❖ **NOTE** Readers who encouter unfamiliar or specialized terms may find definitions in the *Glossary*

LEGS STRIDING — ARMS SWINGING

13 TALES AFOOT

ONE - AFOOT
TOES FOR SEEING

——ONE - AFOOT——
TOES FOR SEEING

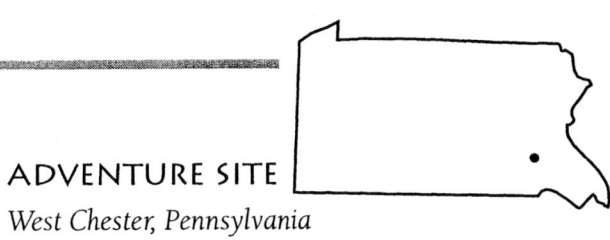

ADVENTURE SITE
West Chester, Pennsylvania

Study the woods, their coniferous and deciduous trees. Are they old or young? Sparse or thick? And if the moon comes out tonight, will its light penetrate the forest canopy?

Study the moon. In what phase is it tonight? New or full? Waxing or waning? What time did it rise last night? Will it rise on schedule, forty minutes later, tonight? Are there clouds that will obscure it? If you go out tonight, will it light your way?

Or will you have to carry a light?

And if you haven't studied the moon, and the forest, and you forget your light, will your feet find their way?

This tale is about my toes' first lesson in seeing.

As the scene opens, I am on the cusp between teen-ager and adult. I am spending the week-end with new friends who own rural property near West Chester, Pennsylvania. A dozen of us have been playing volley-ball at a picnic spot a mile from the house. Between the picnic place and the house is a mile of woods reachable only by a narrow but well-worn path.

Outward bound, I travel with the group. I am lulled by that sense of security one enjoys when others are planning and leading. They know the way; I depend on them instead of memorizing the route.

After the noisy sociability of volley-ball, I seem to be ready for a moment in the company of Mother Nature. When the others leave to return to the farm house, I venture beyond the picnic area, away from the house. I enjoy a walk in the woods. It is summer; no need to worry about a sweater after dark.

I stroll to the place where the path seems to end. I have arrived at a small stream. I listen a while, eavesdropping as the stream whispers to the roots of the trees. The setting sun lights the tree-tops as I turn back toward the picnic area.

On the ground, where I thread my way between tall oaks, tall maples and their small saplings, it is dusk, nearly dark. When I reach the picnic place and try to cross the open area, I nearly walk into the volley-ball net.

Then, in the gathering darkness, I have a bit of trouble finding the path that opens from a corner of the playing area. When I enter the woods again, I begin having a lot of trouble. I become aware immediately that I'll have to *feel* for the right place to plant my feet, for now, in the failing light, I can look down at them and see nothing at all. I begin to be alarmed.

Then I have a thought: *I wonder whether there will be moonlight. Or starlight.* It has been only a little cloudy at sunset; maybe that means there will be stars. I have no idea what phase the moon may be in at the moment. I have not been paying attention to the moon's waxing and waning.

I am feeling my way now. The path is a very dim reality before me, and I seem to be more off it than on. How far off I can't tell. How could I? And now it is completely dark. I cannot see even the giant shapes of tree trunks, much less the tiny twigs at branch-ends that threaten to poke at my now wide-open eyes. I could close my eyes to protect them, but then I couldn't hope to catch even the smallest hint of a shape or a light that might provide some guidance. But wide open or not, my poor weak eyes, far feebler than the owl's or the bob-cat's, now can see nothing — nothing at all. It seems far safer to travel with my eyes closed: less chance of damage from a twig attack.

If I have ever been in this situation before, I can't remember it: in the woods without a light, able to see not even my hand before my face, and needing to walk a mile on an unfamiliar path.

I am aware that my feet will need to do something more than walk. They will need to become sensors of where the path is. How? By telling me what is underfoot. Grass or worn path? Leaves or bare earth? Large stones or little stones?

The small branches hitting me in the chest, arms and face are but a rough indicator of whether I am on course. The better sign is whether the ground is hard or soft under my street shoes.

It is slow going.

Oof! Ouch! I must have walked directly into a big branch. I can't get around this one by putting my hands in my pockets and walking straight ahead. I'll have to go around it. But which way? To the right or the left? Let's try left.

No; that's not it. There are more twigs, and they seem to be higher up. Ouch! That one hurt. Scratched me right on top of the head. Better try going to the right. Maybe back up first. Dern! Another one poked me in the back. Maybe now I can go right. Ah! It seems clear here; and by golly, the ground here feels a bit harder. And to the right it's still clear. Almost a foot of hard ground. Now we're on the path. Forward!

And for three baby steps, carefully taken, I can actually move forward. Then, without warning, my toe seems to strike something hard. Luckily I am not trying to move fast; that one might have hurt.

Let's see. That was the right foot. I'd better move to the left. And, as I move left, my left foot seems to touch harder ground.

But in a moment my right foot strikes a hard object.

A stone in the path? There's hard ground left, right and ahead of it. I must still be on the path.

If I stray to one side or the other, I try not to go very far to the side. The sooner I step back to the path, the less time I'll spend being twigged, scraped and bumped. I am getting the hang of this kind of navigation. I increase my pace. Then —

What's this? Off the path again? Dry leaves crackling underfoot? Now how did that happen all of a sudden? Trying to go too fast. Now! Right or left?

I take a step to the right. Still dry leaves underfoot.

Hmm. Leaves on the path? Suppose I brush them aside with my foot. Is the ground hard underneath? No; soft. Feels like grass. One more step to the left. Still soft. Another?

And the left half of my left foot seems to be on more solid earth. I move it three inches to the left and —

Voila! The path!

At this rate I may get back by midnight.

Inching onward, and often astray, I am sometimes unsure whether I am left or right of the path. I am tempted to become panicky.

What if — Then, after fumbling, my feet cease making crackling sounds and feel the hardness of the beaten track. Slow going; but the principle is sound. *It's a good plan! Then persevere!*

There are only three dimensions: time, space and patience. So I continue in my snail-like pace.

Wait! What was that?

Voices. I open my eyes.

Ah! A light ahead.

The voices and the lights: stimuli for two more of my five senses after navigating with only the skin sense and the kinesthetic.

The ordeal has been brief, and my alarm quite temporary. But the lesson my feet learned on that moonless night has lasted half a century. ❖

—TWO - AFOOT—
Mancos Cañon Side-Winder

—TWO - AFOOT—
MANCOS CAÑON SIDE-WINDER

ADVENTURE SITE
*Mesa Verde National Park
Colorado*

Between my junior and senior years in college I had the opportunity to work a summer in Mesa Verde National Park. For six days each week I made coffee, sandwiches and milk shakes for tourists. I watched my co-workers compete for tips when a Hollywood celebrity or someone equally self-important dropped in at our snack bar.

Off duty I engaged in both serious and frivolous activity. I joined Ranger-led tours of Cliff Palace and Spruce Tree House. I studied the dioramas in the park museum, learning about the vanished Anasazi. I carried on a summer courtship. And with my fellow summer employees, I wrote and helped produce a musical comedy on the apocryphal history of the ancient cliff dwellers of the Mesa Verde. On my days off I went hiking.

I explored the mesa, where I nibbled on piñon nuts. "Nibbled" is the right word, for the tiny, stunted piñon trees produced a sparse crop of tiny, thin-shelled fruit, and the harvesting and cracking probably consumed nearly as many calories as the eating provided.

Itching to range farther afield, I had the benefit of advice from my colleague Johnny, who spent his days sweating over the dish-washing machine in the concession's kitchen. Johnny was an inveterate explorer of the surrounding mesas and cañons. Desert hiking, he claimed, is an art unto itself unlike the art of sauntering in temperate forests. Johnny stressed the need to carry plenty of water, to wear a good hat, to keep one's throat and the back of the neck covered; in fact, to keep all of oneself covered — in wool ! — as protection from both the intense heat of the day and the pervasive chill that comes in quickly after the sun has set. Aside from the hazards posed by the climate, the only danger I might face, Johnny offhandedly remarked, was from rattlers, which in molting season might strike blindly.

"Oh, and by the way, we're just getting into the blind season for rattlesnakes."

I listen intently to this wisdom and absorb a good deal of it. I have the Easterner's great yearning to benefit to the full from this rare exposure to a new and strange Western environment. Especially, I want to view that wonderful stream of which I have heard reports: the Mancos River, said to be eight miles distant. After all, in that dry country, rivers are rare. The cañon beside the Mesa Verde is dry except for a once-a-year cloudburst. In my thinking the general absence of water in my environment lends enchantment to the one river in the area.

To get to the river one descends the Mesa Verde, which rises some hundreds of feet above the cañon floor. Johnny has told me about the best route. I know from casual observation that there are sheer drops — dangerous drops, where mothers constantly worry about their young children's safety. I have looked out of the big window of the snack bar during idle moments and observed the carefree children and the worried mothers. I have heard reports of park guests being injured in falls while scrambling on the edge of the mesa. It is clear to me that finding and adhering to the one safe route down from the mesa is of great importance if my hike is not to end in disaster.

On the morning of my holiday I rise early, not long after sunrise, and take my breakfast in the staff dining room, slipping in and leaving before any of my closest acquaintances can question me about my plans. Only Cliff, the bartender (my tent-mate), and Johnny the dishwasher are privy to my agenda. Someone, I reason, needs to know, "just in case."

Day-pack on my back, canteen slung from my belt, I stride down the asphalt-paved main drive to the point Johnny has indicated, turn off and start climbing down. I soon see that the route he has described is in fact not only the least hazardous; it is the only rational route. The surrounding rock shelves and sheer drops are frightening to behold. When I am five minutes into my careful descent, the narrow, rock-strewn path gives way to a boulder field of gigantic cubes three feet, five feet, eight feet on a side. I find myself wishing for an extra epidermis on my hands to supplement the heavy clothing covering the rest of me; climbing down over these rough, rocky surfaces will be hard on my hands.

And on my backside. Some of the boulders are best traversed by sitting down and easing off. Others call for turning over on my belly, slipping my chest over the edge and groping with my feet for the solid earth or rock below. Sometimes I must hang by my hands and drop a foot or more. Once or twice the thought occurs to me that climbing back up this trail may be as problematic as getting down has proved to be.

After I have labored for twenty minutes to ease my way down through the boulder field, it stops abruptly. I am now on level ground and expect to be for the remainder of the trip. Now I can give minimal attention to placing my feet. I am free to be a tourist.

I have been told that the attentive traveler in the cañon may sometimes find lesser cliff dwellings and even occasional ancient caves and rock paintings. I have already decided to be a keen observer. Other than archaeological sites (and sights), most of the landscape consists of sparse, stunted vegetation and cañon walls in varying degrees of steepness. Except for two small apartment-like stone structures high on the cliff to the right and one dark set of lines which might have been painted by the ancient inhabitants, the archaeological traces are few, unless one counts the small opening perhaps twenty feet up the cliff, looking inaccessible from above or below, which imagination may paint as an ancient dwelling, or at least an overnight refuge. And perhaps the vertical line of ever-so-slight depressions in the cliff to my right served the Anasazi as a ladder. If so, they must have been either very sure-footed or remarkably intrepid — or both!

But these signs are few and widely separated; and the way long and dusty. A dull trip, you may say, except, of course, that I am traveling in country the like of which I have never seen before this summer and may never see again in my lifetime.

I begin to be anxious. I glance occasionally at my watch and, more importantly, at the westwardly progressing sun, which will disappear over the cañon rim long before it sets over the plains or on the mesas. Without the sun, the hot cañon floor under my feet will cool quickly. I do not wish to spend the night here. I am ready for my arrival at the river long before I can actually see the line of trees announcing its presence.

The Mancos River, I find, is no great shakes: a muddy brown stream not over fifteen feet wide and not appearing to be more than a couple of feet deep, lined by a few small cottonwood trees. The river flows along as if it had no very great or impressive mission in life. But the mere fact that there is in this arid land that much water at all, going anywhere, is perhaps impressive enough in itself. I stand a while meditating on these less than profound thoughts. Then I look again at my watch. It is just twelve o'clock.

I find a convenient cottonwood tree, sit leaning against it, work my shoulders out of the day pack and take out my lunch. It does seem surprising to me, as I watch the brown water sliding lazily by, that I have not made better time. I can easily walk four miles an hour; I started descending the mesa about eight o'clock, and I have walked only eight miles, according to Johnny's estimate. Maybe he was wrong; or maybe he's a fast walker. I decide to swallow the rest of my sandwich while walking along. No need to be caught in this cañon with the sun going down. Right now it is high and hot, but when it starts to disappear over the cañon rim —

Heat or not, I quicken my pace. Once or twice I reflect that it might be a good idea to give some regard to where I place my feet, in view of what Johnny has said about side-winders and the rattlers' blind season; but when the narrow path I am walking on enters the shadow of the cañon wall and stays in the shade, my thoughts turn to that other danger: spending the night in the cañon.

Sure enough, dusk descends well before I arrive at the boulder field. I know it will not be simply foolish but really impossible to find my way through the boulders in the dark. Gripped by the beginnings of panic, I start to run. Then, winded and hot, I slow to a walk.

"So what? What's the big deal about spending the night on the cañon floor? I'm warmly enough dressed. In the morning I'll have daylight for climbing boulders and enough time to wash, dress and get to work."

Thinking thus, I proceed more leisurely until it is truly too dark to make safe progress. Stepping off the trail, I look for and soon find a rectangle of ground smooth enough and large enough to accommodate my lanky frame.

Taking off my day pack to use as a pillow, I lie down and prepare to sleep. At first I am comfortably warm. Still, I follow my usual style of napping: stuffing my hands in my pockets. This practice stems from childhood experiences. I would lie in bed listening to the sounds my older brother made as he scraped and cut on his ingrown toenails. Then I would dream blades — all kinds of blades, terrifyingly sharp and threatening. Gripped by this nightmare, I always felt the need to protect my fingernails and toenails from being cut and scraped by that world of blades. In childhood, I protected my twenty nails by burying them in the bedclothes; now, in the cañon, I use my pockets. Safe from blades, I drift off to sleep. From time to time I awaken shivering. Now my hands are in my pockets for another reason: to keep themselves warm.

One particular awakening seems different from the others. I am cold, yes; but it seems that something else is amiss. Something seems to have touched my right sleeve. Indeed, whatever it is doesn't stop at the sleeve but continues across the arm; I can feel a very slight weight on my arm. And whatever it is now seems to be both on my arm and proceeding across my chest. It is evidently a living creature. Indeed, the creature is now clearly gliding smoothly and at the same time feeling sand-papery. Now what creature glides smoothly and feels sand-papery through a wool shirt? Still gliding smoothly, the creature now occupies a band across my entire chest and continues sand-papering along, crossing and descending my other arm in its wave-like motion. What am I to do? What but lie still, as I have been doing? After all, I am a guest here, enjoying the hospitality of someone else's bedroom or, more likely, lying stretched across some wild creature's I-66.

Whoever it is departs. Sleep returns, and light creeps up the sky. I hike to the boulder field and climb it; wash and go to work.

✧

When I was a boy huddled with my siblings around the old Zenith® radio in the living room, one of our heroes on the Tom Mix show was "The Old Wrangler." The Old Wrangler of course never cursed; those were the "good old days" when children's ears were sheltered from the gross and the tasteless. He did, however, occasionally call someone a "cussed mangy side-winder." Like most animal metaphors, that one was not quite just.

Some blessed mangy side-winder had evidently spared me to hike again another day. ❖

—THREE - AFOOT—
BEAR-LY ASLEEP

❖ 26 WILDERNESS ADVENTURES: AFOOT & AFLOAT

—THREE - AFOOT—

BEAR-LY ASLEEP

ADVENTURE SITE
*Balsam Mountain, Great Smoky
Mountains National Park
North Carolina*

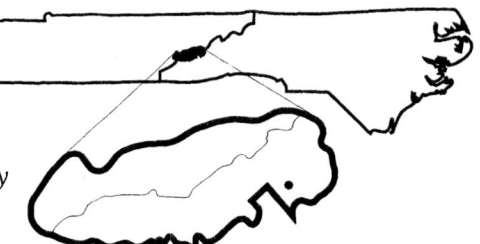

Before the children were born, Diana and I lived in east Tennessee, less than an hour's drive from the Great Smoky Mountains National Park. Often we'd get home from work and, on impulse, pack a picnic supper. Soon we were eating it by a scenic and melodious mountain stream.

Once, during supper, we witnessed a special show: a bear cub wading and playing in the stream. Another time, spending a week-end at Mt. LeCompte Lodge, we were entertained by Mama and Papa Bear raiding the garbage pit. Like other travelers in the Smokies, we were frequently caught in "bear jams." At these times traffic in the park came to a halt, and tourists sat gawking as bears trashed the trash cans and feasted on the garbage.

We were acquainted with bears. We admired and enjoyed them — from a distance. We were perfectly aware — as some park visitors did not seem to be — that bears are wild animals.

❖

Fast-forward in time.

We are now a car-camping family of four. We own a Rambler station wagon. You remember them. Both the front seat and the back could be folded down flat, making the entire interior into a bed. We carry a tent with us but sometimes don't bother with it, particularly when the weather is clear, or we are in a hurry, or it's getting too dark to find and fit the pieces. There is space enough in the payload compartment for two persons: one wife and one toddler (daughter Lydian), and on the front seat enough space for son Reed, an infant. I am Odd Man Out.

We arrive well after dark on a late spring evening at Balsam Mountain Campground (elevation 5340'), on the eastern side of the Great Smoky Mountains National Park. We are tired. We decide not to put up the tent. Since the weather is cool but fine, I roll out a pad and sleeping bag beside (very nearly under) the picnic table. Since many picnickers, unaware of the effect of their leavings on wild life, are careless about scattering food scraps, to settle anywhere in the vicinity of the food service area of a campground is not a good idea. Tid-bits scattered by picnickers tend to attract uninvited night visitors. Some of these may be dangerous.

But it is late, and I am not thinking about that. The drive from home was tiring, and in the evening chill I am thinking only about how good the warm sleeping bag will feel. I give a moment's thought to making myself as inconspicuous as possible, lest the bears decide to pay a call. We know, of course, of the general rule: lock all food — and preferably all food smells — out of reach of wild animals. Following this rule, we make a place for the cooler and the "dry box" inside the station wagon.

Lydian is sleepy and hardly responds to my good-night hug and kiss. Reed is asleep already.

Diana is ready to say "Good-night"; much of the burden of preparation for these expeditions falls to her.

After tucking in the family and saying "Good night," I try to settle down in my meager plot of level ground beside the picnic table. But like any road-weary driver, I have trouble leaving the highway. In that space behind my eyelids, I watch the miles roll by.

While trying to settle, I am aware that other campers up the hill have not yet retired. I hear sounds, most of them from children. After a few sessions in a public campground, one develops some capacity to screen out some of these camping sounds. Natural sounds enhance the outdoor experience; any human sound does the reverse. Some selectivity is essential.

By degrees I become aware of a noisy stir among the campers. It seems that a bear is making its rounds. In fact, as I peek out from the tiny breathing-hole of the sleeping bag, I fancy I can see her (or him) sniffing at a tent up the line. I make myself small, pulling the bag up around my head. In a moment — it seems like a long moment — I hear the bear passing through our campsite, possibly ten yards from my "bed." Fortunately, nothing about my location makes it worth the bear's while to stop and investigate. Mr., or Ms., Bruin lumbers past, twenty feet from my "bed," and continues down the mountain, passing from the campground into the more familiar and comfortable forest.

When I mention my nocturnal visitor to the family at breakfast the next morning, I get little response. We have all met many bears and observed many more without formal introduction. We have grown somewhat accustomed. We refrain from feeding them; and we keep a respectful distance. We have been good guests in their territory. "Live and let live" is our motto.

Fortunately it seems to be the bears' as well. ❖

—FOUR - AFOOT—
Traffic Cop in Linville Gorge

—FOUR - AFOOT—
Traffic Cop in Linville Gorge

ADVENTURE SITE
*Linville Gorge, Pisgah National Forest
North Carolina*

Son Reed is four. He likes to think of himself as a "big boy." One of the things a big boy does is lead.

Parents who wish to raise a "big boy" must meet certain requirements. For one thing, they must let the big boy lead. But before that, they must make him a leader.

We of course have tried to instill in our son a wilderness ethic. We want him to respect the sanctity of wild places and the rights of their denizens. We also want him to take responsibility for the human beings who venture there.

The four of us are strung out along a narrow path in Linville Gorge. To our right the land slopes noticeably upward. On our left the rim of the gorge is only a few yards away, just beyond the trees. Reed is leading, followed by Diana and Lydian. I am bringing up the rear.

Reed halts in mid-step.

"Stop," he says in a quiet but commanding voice, turning toward us and holding up a policeman-like hand.

Across the trail in front of him, with deliberate speed, moves a six-foot-long, three-inches-thick black snake, still a bit torpid from its long winter dormancy. Though it is not speeding, only a moment elapses between its emergence from the tall grass on the uphill side of the trail and its disappearance on the lower side. Both the appearance and the disappearance seem sudden. Our host in this wilderness, which we visit under sufferance, has revealed herself or himself for but a moment.

"Okay," Reed says, when the snake is out of sight among the leaves and tall grass. Motioning for us to follow, he turns and coolly leads us on down the narrow path. ❖

—FIVE - AFOOT—
A True - Life Adventure Atop Mt. Sterling

— FIVE - AFOOT —

A True-Life Adventure Atop Mt. Sterling

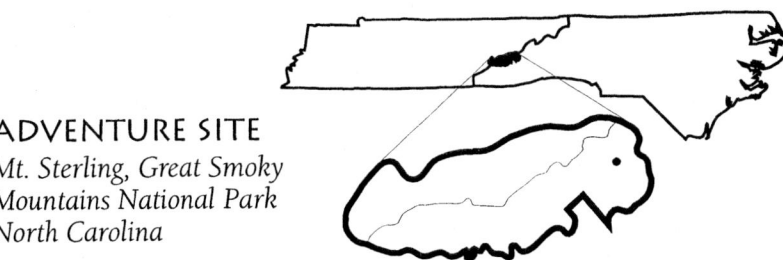

ADVENTURE SITE
*Mt. Sterling, Great Smoky Mountains National Park
North Carolina*

When my young family began to emerge from the Rambler into a tent, we often pitched it beside Cataloochee Creek, on the eastern edge of the Great Smoky Mountains National Park. If we got bored with hanging out in the deep shade creekside or wished to get away from fisherpersons for a while, we piled into the station wagon and drove more deeply into the Park. Traveling northwesterly on a government road that wound upstream paralleling Little Cataloochee Creek, we soon discovered Sterling Gap. Seeing the sign identifying the trail to Mt. Sterling (elevation 5,835 feet), we yearned to climb it and check the view from the top.

One fine day we park the station wagon at the Gap and take off on foot, equipped with food and water and shod in what will have to pass as hiking boots. The trail is broad and rocky; horses are permitted on it, traveling in small groups, led by a wrangler. We have noticed signs advertising the stables in Cataloochee Valley and have resolved to patronize them "some day." In the meantime, we make do with Shank's Mare, envying the riders each time a party of horses comes by.

The children, ages four and six, are game but tire easily and require frequent piggy-back relief, especially when the trail becomes long and the summit seems ever more elusive.

Eventually, though, we emerge into a grassy meadow, where we figure out that the odd structure there, unlike any we have seen before, is a fancy, complicated series of hitching rails for parties of horses such as we have been seeing.

A small cabin has a stone doorstep that invites sitters; but if one climbs a bit farther, up a gentle grassy incline, one can undertake a more dramatic climb: up the winding steps of Mt. Sterling fire-tower, which commands a glorious view of the surrounding mountains and valleys. Diana sits. I proceed. Now that we have attained the summit, she and the children may do as they like, short of endangering themselves. I opt for the vista.

The children, who a moment ago were too tired to plod up the trail, now follow me up the winding stairs, not without admonitions of caution from Mama.

I can linger over the view from a commanding height. No situation is more conducive to fresh thoughts, deep breaths and even profound and inspiring meditation.

To the northeast we can see Mt. Cammerer; to the north Peaked Knob, Snowbird and Buzzard Roost. Grassy Knob lies northeasterly, Canadian Top (elev. 4,118 feet) southeasterly; and to the south, Big Cataloochee Mountain, its top 4,122 feet above the sea. It is a scene to lift one's thoughts. The children climb and descend the tower. Diana calls out a caution but does not come up.

Amidst this scene I observe something else, on the ground below me as I stand on the topmost platform. I whisper quietly to the children.

"Lydian! Reed! Come on up here!"

"What?"

"What is it, Dad?"

"Shhh! Come here. Look."

Sixty feet below us a young cottontail is fleeing danger. The menacing pursuer is a long, lithe creature: a weasel, the first I have ever seen in the wild. It, too, must be a young one; surely a more experienced hunter would long since have overtaken its quarry and made a quick meal of it. But the bunny seems to be holding its own. It is visible for a moment and then disappears in the yard-high shrubs at the foot of the tower, seemingly confusing the weasel and eluding it for the moment. Then the cottontail appears again a few yards away, visible momentarily through a gap in the rank plant growth and then out of sight again; and a moment later the weasel crosses the gap where we have just seen the rabbit.

This mortal chase continues on the same pattern: the weasel gets close to the rabbit; the rabbit executes some maneuver which seems to confuse the weasel long enough to allow the rabbit to escape — temporarily — perhaps until the rabbit tires or until the young weasel is relieved or assisted by a more mature hunter.

The chase goes on for what seems like an hour but is probably closer to ten minutes, during which I have no trouble at all quieting the children, so fascinated are they. We leave the mountain before the conclusion of this true-life adventure.

❖

This scene may have vanished from my children's memories, but I daresay their bones and viscera have not forgotten. ❖

— SIX - AFOOT —
Brown Bears and Blueberries

—SIX - AFOOT—
Brown Bears and Blueberries

ADVENTURE SITE
Appalachian Trail, near Clingman's Dome, Tennessee

Reed and Lydian are now six and nine years old. Their mother and I are no longer a couple. My bonding time with the children is spent largely in the outdoors. This week-end we decide to hike a portion of the Appalachian Trail, a short section between Clingman's Dome and Siler's Bald. Clingman's Dome, after decades of feuding by Tennessee and North Carolina, has taken its place as the highest peak in the state of Tennessee and second highest in the Eastern United States, Mt. Mitchell the highest.

On a sunny Saturday morning we head westward on a broad but narrowing trail leading mostly downhill from Clingman's summit. We plan to spend the night at the first available lean-to, not more than four or five miles away. It is a kind of shake-down overnighter, one of many such to follow. I have an overnight-capacity rucksack which carries at least the load of a proper external-frame back-pack. Each of the children is carrying personal gear in a substantial day-pack.

Our tranquil enjoyment of the scene around us is disturbed by sounds approaching from behind. The voices quickly become quite loud, and in a moment we are overtaken by a noisy troop of boy scouts. A dozen boys varying in age between nine and fourteen appear out of the woods, a young scout master and a middle-aged one struggling to keep up.

"Excuse me!"

"Pardon me, sir!"

"Comin' through!"

In the moment that it takes them to pass, we manage to strike up a brief conversation with the younger leader. The boys, it seems, are bent on getting from Clingman's Dome to Fontana Lake in record time. In a moment nothing of them remains but animated conversation, becoming less and less distinct as it recedes into the distance. This crew, I reflect ruefully, is setting a bad example for my children who, I hope, are learning to experience the outdoor world in a somewhat more deliberate and receptive manner. When distance and the acoustical trees dampen the shouts and laughter of the scout troop, and silence reigns once more, the lacy hemlock trees seem more alive, the moss on the rocks more pillowy, the trail ahead more quietly inviting. Passing through a hemlock grove, we step off the trail briefly to study the damage done, presumably, by feral pigs digging in the soft earth for tasty, nourishing roots.

At about four o'clock in the afternoon we arrive at the lean-to which is our destination. The shelter, no doubt built by local Appalachian Trail Club volunteers, is empty, or appears to be. We prepare and eat a leisurely supper, careful not to scatter more crumbs than necessary. We do not wish to train the small creatures to depend on human beings' leavings all summer and, when winter comes, find that they have forgotten how to forage for themselves in the wild. We hang our food pack from a line suspended between trees and use the time between supper and nightfall in examining the lean-to and looking around at the trees, shrubs and wild flowers. When the light in the west has faded, and our energy with it, we bed down in the rude, three-sided shelter.

Now we discover that our temporary home is the permanent dwelling of a colony of field mice. At supper we have been careful about crumbs and other left-overs and thus have had no direct contact with these small creatures. Now we have the dubious pleasure of listening to the pitter-patter of their little feet up and down the walls and over the roof. We wonder whether they will pay us a visit.

"Are they going to crawl in bed with us, Dad?" Reed wants to know.

"I don't think so, Son. I think they're afraid of us."

Nevertheless I place Reed in the middle, between Lydian and me. Lydian is as close to fearless as any nine-year-old I know. But I have visions of the small four-footed rodents trying to nestle with us in our warm sleeping bags or tear at them in the night for material to build their own little nests.

"They won't bite, will they, Dad?" Lydian wants to know.

"If they do, Sweetie, you bite 'em back."

Finally, and fitfully, we sleep.

On Sunday morning, after our breakfast of water, oranges, hard-boiled eggs and handfuls of granola and G.O.R.P., we shoulder our packs to start back. We have not gone far when, enticed by some luscious-looking wild blueberries, we turn off the trail to the right and begin our second breakfast. Picking the fat berries and popping them in our mouths, we work our way through the bush with little conversation, forgetting the old woodsmen's advice about the best way to ward off bears.

"Make a noise," they tell us. "Sing and shout." Really, that's not my idea of how to enjoy the wilderness, but maybe it works.

We round a copse. I have heard no sound, but now on the periphery of my vision I detect a slight movement. It seems that we are not the only blueberry lovers present. A big brown bear is feeding fifty feet ahead of us.

"Well, children," I say, as casually and conversationally as feasible, "I think we have had enough berries."

"Why, Dad?" Reed wants to know.

"Mr. Bear would like to have the blueberry patch all to himself."

"Uh-oh!" says Lydian, seeing the bear. "Okay, Mr. Bear."

We retreat to the trail. The bear pays us scant attention as it continues feeding. ❖

—SEVEN - AFOOT—
MITCHELL FALLS INITIATION

Mitchell Falls Initiation
— Seven - Afoot —

ADVENTURE SITE
*Mt. Mitchell State Park
North Carolina*

Unfortunately, the hike described here could probably not be repeated today. Despite the wishes and efforts of park authorities, it has been impossible for the state to acquire the land between Mt. Mitchell summit and Mitchell Falls, an area that has now been developed as a private hunting preserve, according to park personnel. When I hiked with a Sierra Club acquaintance from the base of the mountain to Mitchell Falls a decade after the trip described here, I obtained permission from the owners. Such permission is today highly problematical.

— *F.A.*

In some cultures a definite line is drawn between childhood and adulthood. In East Africa, where Reed was conceived and where Lydian spent two years of toddlerdom, the transition was marked by circumcision rites. Every couple of years the village *shaman* gathered up the young boys who had reached puberty, took them into the forest and taught them what a man in that culture needed to know. He also circumcised each boy using a sharp stone or possibly his less-than-sterile pocket knife. Nowadays there is a movement toward either doing away with these rites entirely or performing them in a hospital or other aseptic environment.

In our society there is no clear line between childhood and adulthood. *Bar mitzvah* is something like it; "coming out" is something like it; graduation from high school or college is something like it; arriving at driving or voting age is something like it; but there is nothing really quite like it. As a result, a young person may no longer be young when she or he "arrives" at adulthood and begins functioning as a fully fledged citizen.

I recall vividly the occasion when, in my view, my daughter showed her mettle and my son "came of age." It was the day (and night) of our hike from Mt. Mitchell summit to Mitchell Falls.

The hike was not my children's idea; it was mine. Lydian was willing to join me on condition that we include her pal Mary in the trip. When Reed made a similar request, I had to turn him down on the basis of the limited capacity of the vehicle (really, it was the limited capacity of Dad to cope with another youngster on this slightly hazardous adventure). All three children showed true grit that day — and night: courage, forbearance and responsibility — traits which seem to me to mark the difference between child and adult. Surely those are traits which any initiation ceremony, whether circumcision rites, sorority initiation or passing a driving test, is designed to foster.

Mt. Mitchell State Park consists of 1,469 acres of forest surrounding the highest peak in Eastern United States (elevation 6,684 feet). It may be hot summer outside the Black Mountains, but atop Mt. Mitchell, there is always a breeze that is at least cool even in the hot summer and in winter is frigid in the extreme, as the meteorological displays in the museum dramatically demonstrate.

The Park, established in 1915 as the first state park in North Carolina, commemorates the life and work of Elisha Mitchell, a science professor at the University of North Carolina. For many years Prof. Mitchell spent his time away from the classroom hiking, exploring and studying in the wilderness surrounding the mountain and the park which now bear his name. Elisha Mitchell met his death, evidently, by falling from a cliff above 40-foot-high Mitchell Falls. His body was found at the base of the water-drop. For a long time I was curious to see the waterfall which enticed Prof. Mitchell to take a final, lethal risk.

Unfortunately our Mitchell Falls outing met with a series of unforeseen setbacks, though none so catastrophic as Elisha Mitchell's. First, the "limited camp" in the park (half a mile from the summit) had reached its limit and had no place for us when we arrived Friday night. The closest legal camping place was thirty miles back toward home, in the town of Cherokee. We had to "make do" by backtracking down the mountain to an illegal and inadequate bivouac in a wayside park. Then the next morning, after we'd spent a less than comfortable night and driven for half an hour back to the summit, the ranger discouraged us by indicating that Mitchell Falls was outside the boundaries of the park and that the trail was not well blazed, had not been maintained and was likely to be overgrown. Nevertheless, we started out about nine o'clock in the morning with an optimistic outlook and every hope that we'd have time, light and energy to get to the falls and back to the summit before darkness set in. I had no desire to spend the night on the highest peak in Eastern United States with three young children, one of them not my own. But I felt we had time to make the mere six-mile round trip which, admittedly, was virtually straight down and then straight up over an ill-marked trail. We were on a tight timetable, but we were determined to have a wonderful adventure in the Great Out-of-Doors.

The trail from the summit to the falls starts in the parking lot. We walk down the main paved road to a point where a path to the right passes down through a picnic area. Below the picnic area a narrow trail heads sharply downhill for a couple of miles. Reed wants to lead. He enjoys playing the "big boy."

We reach the old railroad right-of-way which girdles the mountain.

"Which way do we go, Dad?"

"Turn right. No you see the sun behind us?"

"Yep. Peeping through the trees."

"Then that must be east. We want to go north for a brief spell. We'll be following an old logging railroad right-of-way. You remember what the ranger said?"

"Yep. I heard it all. Are you worried about finding blazes?"

"No. I don't think so. We just have to look sharp. They may be faded, and some of the trees with blazes on them may have fallen since the trail was last maintained."

"Are we looking for blazes now?"

"Maybe not. Our next turn, remember, will be left, off this road."

Reed is the one who notices the pile of stones at the left edge of the road, marking the trail that now plunges off the right-of-way and straight down the mountain. He continues leading as we turn and follow in single file, digging in our heels as we begin our sharp descent. The trail no longer has much claim to the name. With each step only the back half of the foot strikes the earth, which is here a loose black humus. Our hiking boots are filling with it.

The old saying comes to mind in reverse: "What goes down must come back up." If our knees are working hard now as brakes, our thighs will soon labor mightily as lifters.

"Oh, no!" escapes from me before I can censor it. Reed stops in his tracks.

"What's the matter?" Lydian wants to know. Mary is silent. As guest, she seems reluctant to claim a voice in deliberations.

"How long's it been, Reed, since you've seen a blaze?"

"I don't know," Reed says, "but this looks like a trail. It's clearer than the rest of the woods."

"Trouble is," I say, "nothing looks much like a trail."

"Are we lost, Dad?" Lydian asks. Again Mary, as guest, too polite to interfere in matters of policy, says nothing and reveals no emotion. Her silence and dead-pan stoicism are some comfort. I do not need to cope with hysterical children, especially others' children.

"No," I respond; and I think I am being honest; "we're not lost, but it seems that the trail is."

"Can we find the falls without the trail?" Lydian asks.

I do not answer. I do not know.

We pass through more thick forest. Then, as the forest thins, the rocks become more numerous and the footing more hazardous. Holes from which rocks have been dislodged are often filled with leaves, which conceal them, inviting an ankle to drop in for a sprain.

"Listen!" says Reed, holding up a hand to bring us to an observant halt.

"By golly, I can hear water," I say. "If this isn't the falls, at least it's the creek."

"If we follow the sound," Reed reasons, "we'll reach the falls; right?"

"I reckon so. Let's stop and have lunch."

Though it is July, we are actually cool sitting in the shade overlooking the ravine where we feel sure Mitchell Creek is running unseen somewhere below. I have been wearing my extra wool shirt around my waist but put it on during lunch. The girls take out sweaters from their day packs, and I pass around sandwiches, which have kept their shape pretty well, packed in coffee cans.

"What time is it, Dad?" Lydian asks.

"Eleven o'clock. At the rate we're traveling, we'll reach the falls by noon. Then we'll have at least seven hours of daylight left for hiking back."

"What will happen if we can't find the trail?"

The question has occurred to me, and I have not enjoyed thinking about it. It will be cold; it will be damp; and all we have is our lunch: no sleeping bags, no rain gear, no supper, not even matches to build a fire. Even in July, we could encounter more exposure to the elements than we've bargained for.

That is what I'm thinking. What I say is: "We ought to be able to pick up the trail when we reach the falls."

The sound of the creek is elusive. For a few minutes it is distinct. It seems to be coming from the right as we pick our way carefully downward over the moss-covered, loosely-seated small rocks. I can feel my son's trust. He knows my philosophy about experiences and their importance. If you pick them carefully and put enough of them together, you build character. Possibly Reed has but a vague idea of what character is, but the teachers in school talk enough about it to give him the idea that it is mighty important.

I stop and look around. It is beautiful: dark, the trees so tall it is hard to find the tops, which are blocking out the sunlight. And it is hard to see that those leaves up there are connected to the trunks right here beside us, which are holding the soils and blocking the rocks in their slide down the mountain. Plants are scarce: galax, oxalis, moss, widely dispersed. There is something important here which it is hard to define. Moss patterns on the north sides of trees? The huge and the small fungi of all shapes, growing in unexpected places? Or is it ourselves? The patience required to keep putting one foot before the other? I wonder, standing in this remote and beautiful place, whether the children have any idea of the meaning of this experience to them — and to the growth of character.

On down the mountain we plunge, our heels sinking into the black earth with each step or slipping on small stones and threatening to land us on our bottoms — or head over heels.

And then, look! There it is.

Or is it?

Is that Mitchell Falls — that thin stream of water splashing and spurting down the face of a sloping wall of rock? We four stand on a small gravel bar looking up. To me the rock looks at least sixty feet tall.

"There it is."

"Are you sure, Dad?"

"Pretty sure."

We stand for a moment contemplating this wonder. We are on a small round sand bar within the stream bed beside a clear pool perhaps ten feet in diameter. Into it splashes a thin stream of water which in its falling has made the rock glisten. It looks to me like the kind of place I'd try to climb to take a shortcut if I were Elisha Mitchell racing nightfall. Look at the rhododendron on both sides of the rock face. So thick you'd never get through it bushwhacking with a machete.

"If I had it to do, I'd certainly try to go right up the middle instead of trying to push through the thick rhododendron. In fact, it might be worth a try when we start back up."

"No, Dad!" Lydian is alarmed. I have actually placed both hands and one foot on the slippery surface and tested it for climbing. "Remember what happened to Elisha Mitchell," she says, her voice pleading.

I step back and study the falls and the adjacent rhododendron-covered rocks.

"What are you thinking, Dad?" Reed wants to know.

"Well, there's no sign of a trail on either bank. I was hoping there would be, but there isn't. In fact, I don't believe I could tell you how we came into this stream bed. It looks to me from here as if there were no way out of it, but of course that can't be so. If there's a way in, there has to be a way out. There seems no way to walk through these rhododendron; they're too thick; but why not climb over them — use them like a ladder? They go just about straight up."

"I suppose they're better to climb on than the slippery rocks are," Reed says.

"Let's go, then." And I start pulling myself up by grasping the branches of the rhododendron and trying to grip with the deeply grooved rubber soles of my hiking boots. It isn't easy; the branches are slippery, and though my hands are holding well, my boots aren't able to. Also, it is hard to stay *outside* of the mass of branches; the branches want to draw me into their midst, but not close enough to gain a foothold on the rock surface in which they are somehow rooted.

"Dad!" Lydian now sounds downright distressed. In her voice is a note I know well from long association. It has come through to me in moments of crisis as through a special private daughter-father pipeline that is always present, though rarely utilized and never acknowledged.

"Okay, Sweetie. I'm coming down."

One option now remains: going back the way we came — if we can find it.

Between Reed and me there is tacit agreement that I will lead. His leadership has got us off the trail; mine may get us back to where we started.

May.

But before fifteen minutes have passed, we find ourselves in a thick stand of rhododendron, which seems to thwart our progress in the only direction in which we want to go: up. Progress through the rhododendron goes like this: raise knees; step up. Simultaneously reach hands forward, grasping and parting the inch-thick trunks or branches immediately ahead. Thrust one shoulder through the gap, following it with the other, no matter how much skin one scrapes off back or chest in the process.

"Do you think we could rest, Dad?" Lydian again.

"Better not, Sweetie. We'd better keep going." I try to sound casual but am not convinced that my tone has reassured the children.

"Are we lost, Dad?" Reed asks.

"Same answer, Son. We're not lost; the trail is. As long as we keep raising our knees and putting one foot forward and above the other, we'll reach the top. These rhododendron can't go on forever."

And of course they don't. By raising our knees and putting one foot forward and above the other, we arrive at the old railroad right-of-way. Now we know we are back on the trail. The turn-off up to and through the picnic area to the summit is not hard to identify. It is inside the park and thus is well marked.

It is dusk when we regain the summit. The six-mile round trip has taken us eleven hours. But we have found the site of old Elisha Mitchell's demise.

Reed starts yawning as soon as we reach the car. The girls choose to lie down on the mattress and sleeping bags in the payload area in back. They have every right to be tired. They have been heroic beyond the usual requirements for teen-aged girls; and now they are opting for gossip and a slumber party. It is clear that the children are in no condition to put up a tent or tolerate more "roughing it," and, to be honest, I am not exactly enthusiastic about the idea myself. Therefore I propose driving to Asheville, finding a late supper and spending the night in a motel. The plan is enthusiastically endorsed. Reed, without a male age-mate and still feeling heroic — and knowing I may be too sleepy to stay awake without his help — decides I might welcome some conversation as we drive down the mountain. Never mind that he is as sleepy as the girls are; he seems to sense a duty to stay with Dad through a continuing trial.

Arriving in Asheville, we stop at the first likely-looking motel to wash off a layer or so of Mt. Mitchell humus. We leave the key at the front desk as we head out to find a restaurant. It is already eleven o'clock. We are tired and hungry.

After supper, as we get back into the car, Reed asks, "Do you think you can find your way back to the motel?"

"Sure. By the way, what was the name of that place?"

"I don't know. Isn't it on the key?"

"Probably, but I left the key at the desk. Well, I'm sure it's down this way."

But it's not down that way. Nor the next way we try. Nor the next. Reed is very sleepy now, and the girls are dozing in back, but he stays alert, helping me play detective. Several of his ideas are ingenious but fruitless, and it is finally my idea that works.

"Let's ask a policemen which way we came into the city when we first arrived; and then drive that way and see if we can figure it out."

It works. By the time it does, Reed is almost asleep but is determined to be good company until the problem is solved and sleeping is a respectable course of action for a self-respecting kid. He is so near sleep when we enter the motel room that my voice startles him.

"I'm proud of you, Son. Not yet twelve years old, and acted like a man." ❖

—EIGHT - AFOOT—
IDYLL ON BULL ISLAND

— EIGHT - AFOOT —
IDYLL ON BULL ISLAND

ADVENTURE SITE
Cape Romain National Wildlife Refuge, South Carolina

I include the following slim record of an island idyll not because it contains any marvelously evocative images of the setting, or any great and wonderful adventures, but for almost purely sentimental reasons. When I think of this trip, it brings into my heart a feeling of pure joy, remembering a serene, unhurried day of sharing with my son the direct enjoyment of nature, unfettered by responsibilities, unsullied by social demands, unpolluted by human greed and commercialism. In short, to remember Bull Island is to evoke a sliver of Paradise to supplement the daily bread of ordinary life.

Carol, bless her heart, a devoted Sierra Club officer and trip leader, had the imagination and initiative to find and to offer the Club adventures to all sorts of wonderful, out-of-the-way places. Bull Island was one of these.

Would you like to visit a sub-tropical paradise devoid of all traces of human beings? Visit Bull Island.

You'll have to charter a boat to get there. Although our small group of Sierra Club adventurers, under Carol's leadership, floated under petro-power to get to the island, I include this trip as a trip on foot, because once on the island, it was our feet that carried us if we wished to explore the turf.

Bull is a barrier island several miles off the coast, about 17 miles north of Charleston, South Carolina, part of the Cape Romain National Wildlife Refuge. Like other barrier islands, it is sometimes the scene of an annual event in the life of the giant sea turtle.

On moonlit nights, especially at the full moon, the females come ashore long enough to dig a deep hole in the sand high on the beach, deposit 100 or so eggs, cover them and, moving on their clumsy, ocean-swimming flippers, plod back to the safety of the sea.

When the young hatch, they instinctively head toward the brightest open horizon. Under normal conditions (pre-*Homo sapiens*), this brightest open horizon was the sea.

The proliferation of cities, resorts, housing developments and other human structures along the coast, and especially the lights of these places, tend to confuse the hatchlings as they try to head out to sea. For this reason visitors to wildlife preserves along the coast are asked to limit their activities at night and especially to avoid showing lights that would misdirect the turtles, which are already drastically limited in their choice of nesting areas.

We arrive in a caravan of three cars at a private dock, where we load our camping gear on a 20-foot launch. After brief consultation between Carol and the owner-skipper, the small launch chugs out into the Intracoastal Waterway.

There's Carol, the impresario, the organizer of this outing, standing with the skipper, he with his hands on the wheel. The two of them face forward as the boat leaves the dock and makes a broad arc to follow the Waterway — briefly. Leaving it, the launch threads its way through broad and narrow passages between vast areas of marsh grass and then across the open water of Bull Bay. Now we are all facing forward, into the wind, our hair flying astern.

It is past time for a late lunch when we arrive on the island and hungrily open our packs before setting up tents. Then it is *ad lib* adventure time.

Reed, a fun-loving, gregarious pre-teen, might have preferred to be somewhere else than on an unpopulated island (humanly speaking) — say, at a party with his peers; but he has enough natural curiosity (somehow it hasn't been bored out of him by his parents, teachers or other adults) to enter into our exploration of the island with some enthusiasm.

Luckily, there are enough hazards and oddities in this place to keep life interesting for the two half-days of our visit. Bull is an island twelve miles long and half that width. We choose to spend our Saturday afternoon exploring the central portion: the semi-tropical forest that runs down the island's center.

One of our first stops is a blind at a fresh-water pond. Since it is summer, we observe but a few species of water-fowl; in spring or fall we would be able to spend many hours peeking through the openings in the thatched walls with binoculars in one hand and bird book in the other. We stay a few minutes, seeing many species we have not known before and some which we have: pied-billed grebe *(Podilymbus podiceps);* double-crested cormorant *(Phalacrocorax auritus);* mallards *(Anas platyrhynoos);* several Canada geese *(Branta canadensis)* and a pair of the vanishing breed of American black ducks *(Anas rubripes),* which are not black at all but sooty brown with a tiny violet-colored wing patch, the male and female looking very much alike (I reckon the two we are seeing are mates).

Reed is only a little impatient; the novelty of seeing even this small concentration of marine avians puts a bit of glue under his shoes.

We pass on south through the central core of woods, following what feels like a trail. It leads us between what appear to be fresh-water lagoons, where —

thrill ! thrill ! — we fancy we are seeing from a distance a long, dark shape that is mighty like an alligator ! Sure enough! And it does not seem to be in any hurry to splash back into the water; nor are we eager to pass close to it, though we have little choice if we wish to follow the sandy dune separating two watery areas. Luckily, we do not have to test whether we can outrun the big bull. It's hot; he's feeling lazy. Maybe he's just enjoyed a heavy meal.

Soon water and dune give way to scrub forest, which occasionally almost resembles climax forest. Tropical palms and palmettos alternate with deciduous oaks and maples. Here we observe something which I have never seen before: black squirrels. I have since read somewhere that these are, taxonomically speaking, gray squirrels (*Sciurus carolinensis*), differentiated in coloration by virtue of unique soil conditions and isolation. Unfortunately, my massive *Encyclopedia of Mammals* does not shed much light on this amazing phenomenon; nor does Barkalow and Shorten's *The World of the Gray Squirrel* (1973), which discusses melanism in squirrels as a genetic phenomenon and lists several states from Minnesota to Virginia — but not North or South Carolina — where black squirrels have been found.

We do not walk to the end of the island but start back to our campsite when we have used up about half the available time between lunch and supper.

After supper — in fact just about the time when I am thinking seriously about testing the hardness of the sand through the tent floor and the capability of my sleeping pad to lessen the same — we begin to hear human sounds. They seem to be coming from the vicinity of the other tents. Soon we note the play of many flashlight beams, as of a party of a dozen or so persons making their way up the trail to the beach on the ocean side.

None of our business, probably. Anyway, we have been admonished by the ranger to stay away from the beach at night to avoid shining lights that might confuse the sea turtles.

In the morning Reed and I hike to the ocean-facing beach and turn left, toward the island's northern tip. All along the beach we find skeletons of trees uprooted by incoming waves and forming a kind of obstacle course through which we wind with much climbing, leaping and stooping.

After exploring the wave-desolated northern beach, we make our way back south, past the trail to camp, in order to reconnoiter the south portion of the Atlantic-facing shore. Here we find the best playground of the trip: a tall tree with a suspended vine that makes a wonderful swing. We linger here for an hour, playing like two young children, taking each other's pictures, trying to outdo one another in foolish bravado and high-swinging grace, flying far out from the tall maple tree and dropping to the soft, forgiving sand.

On Sunday afternoon, headed back to the mainland in the launch, we piece together through overheard bits of conversation the tale of last night's mysterious hunting party. The group, in violation of the Fish and Wildlife Service's prohibitions against night forays, has headed toward the beach to look for egg-laying activity of the giant sea turtles.

✧

Would I have joined the party if invited? Would curiosity and peer pressure have outweighed my concern for the future of the noble and stoutly deck-plated but ecologically vulnerable giant? Probably not; maybe that's why I wasn't invited.

Anyway, I have yet to witness the coming ashore of the giant sea turtle or the blindly instinctive march down the beach and setting off to sea of a new brood of hatchlings. ❖

— NINE - AFOOT —
COMIN' 'ROUND MT. ROGERS

—NINE - AFOOT—
COMIN' 'ROUND MT. ROGERS

ADVENTURE SITE
Mt. Rogers National Recreation Area
Virginia

Brad was one of my favorite outings leaders, and I know why.

It wasn't just because he was successor to Carol (the Carol of Trips "**Eight - Afoot**" and "**One - Afloat**") as chair of the Central Piedmont Group of the Sierra Club, and it wasn't because I sat in the back seat of Carol's car on the way to an outing and listened as Carol briefed Brad on the responsibilities of that office. It wasn't even because Brad brought along on outings his fiancée, who always formed an attractive and pleasant portion of the scenery, or because he lent me an aluminum blanket once when I was shivering in my old army surplus sleeping bag. No, it wasn't for any of these reasons.

It was because he always did his homework before any outing. He always knew exactly where he was going, what he'd find when he got there and what to do if things didn't turn out as expected. He was well prepared because (1) he possessed a vast library of topographic maps; (2) he studied them conscientiously and (3) he scouted each new area before undertaking to lead others into it. Thus I was always willing to go with him on an outing.

To give one example: when we hiked a particular trail, Brad always seemed to know where the springs were. Not everyone can be depended on to bring along enough drinking water, and if anyone had a need to fill a canteen, Brad would consult his map and say, "A half-mile up the trail there's a ravine; and about 100 yards down there's a spring." And then, since he was a lawyer and didn't want to get caught in an error, he'd add: "It was flowing the last time I was here at about three gallons a minute, but that was after a couple of days of rain."

Another example: he studied weather patterns. He had a keen sense of how a particular weather system would affect a mountain or a valley in the same general area. A high place might be affected in one way, a nearby valley in a different way. The west side of a mountain might bear the brunt of a storm, while the sheltered east might have far less rain or snow — or none at all. Thus he was far less prone than other outings leaders to call off a hike just because the weather report for a region predicted severe weather. It was from

Brad, more than from any other outings leader, that I imbibed the principle: *Don't call off the hike until you get to the trailhead and there's a blizzard or a hurricane.* Many a wonderful opportunity has been lost forever because a leader made premature assumptions about the weather. Brad adopted a "Wait and see" or "Adapt and cope" attitude.

I remember one back-packing week-end in particular because it illustrates what I've been saying. I can't pin down precisely where we went because, like most others who traveled with Brad, I left the planning and leading to him. Like others, I let my attention turn to the pure enjoyment of the natural beauty and uniqueness of whatever area Brad chose to explore.

✧

We are to hike to and camp on the summit of Mt. Rogers, the highest peak in the state of Virginia (elev. 5729 feet). The night before the outing, it snowed in southwest Virginia. Does Brad call off the outing? He does not. We proceed as if all were well, as indeed it is. It is late November. There are at least four inches of snow on the ground at the trailhead, and it is still snowing. Nevertheless, we gear up and hit the trail, packs on our backs. A couple of miles up the trail we stop at an old apple orchard for a lunch break. Someone hangs a tarp under some trees to keep snow from collecting too heavily on our heads as we stand munching.

While we are there, a couple of hikers come tramping down the trail, their hats, boots and most of the rest of them crusted with snow. They have spent the night on the summit.

"Six inches of snow," they report, "and we nearly froze." Brad listens thoughtfully to their report of sub-zero temperatures and treacherous conditions underfoot. Then he herds us back down the trail and into the vehicles for a short trip around to the south side of the mountain, where we find —

No snow.

None at all.

Cold weather, but no snow.

We get out of the vehicles a second time and hike to another camping place that Brad is familiar with. We set up camp and spend the night. The next day we enjoy a pleasant hike — in cold but not Arctic conditions, and not through snow. Then we head home, none of us having suffered frostbite or any other severe discomfort: a perfectly enjoyable week-end despite dire weather prognostications.

✧

It may even have been on this trip that I introduced my companions to a newly-discovered and valuable bit of outdoor camping technique: a dual-purpose method of folding a tarp (with modifications, this method works for a tent, air mattress or other item from which it is difficult to squeeze the last remaining air prior to stuffing into its sack for the trip home). Using my handy-dandy method, you will find it easy to make items fit into their original carrying sacks or occupy minimum space in pack or duffel. Here are the instructions:

1) Select the most attractive member of the opposite gender, or the person in the group whom you would most enjoy knowing a bit better.
2) Urgently but politely request that person's help in folding your unwieldy 16-foot by 24-foot tarpaulin.
3) Grasp the two corners of the shorter dimension of the tarp and request your partner do the same at the other end.
4) Stand far enough from your colleague to stretch the tarp to its full extent.
5) Fold the tarp lengthwise.
6) Do it again as often as needed to arrive at a width of 12 inches or other desired dimension.
7) Now walk toward your partner, bringing your end of the tarp up to meet hers (or his).
8) Let him (or her) hold both ends; you pick up the folded end and walk back to stretch it out.
9) Repeat Step 8 as often as necessary to arrive at a folded tarp about 1 foot square (or other desired dimension). You will note that there remains a lot of air trapped in the folds of the tarp. Never fear. The next step will take care of that.
10) Walk toward your helper until the two of you are in position for a very close tango. Place the tarp between you.
11) With the tarp between you, give that partner a grand bear-hug, and squeeze until the air has escaped completely, or until the joke has grown stale or your unwilling victim has had enough.

You can see that this operation serves the dual purposes of getting the air out of the tarp and the strangeness out of the atmosphere between you and your new outdoor friend.

So you may take away from the reading of this **Trip** not only a pointer from me on camping technique but also wisdom from Brad concerning trip planning and strategy: "Wait and see; adapt and cope."

Not to follow my suggestion is to endanger your reputation as an opportunist; not to follow Brad's philosophy is to miss many a once-in-a-lifetime adventure. ❖

—TEN - AFOOT—
HARPER BY MOONLIGHT

—TEN - AFOOT—
HARPER BY MOONLIGHT

ADVENTURE SITE
Harper Creek Wilderness
North Carolina

Too few persons in our removed-from-nature civilization have any notion of the influence of the moon on tides, on animals' behavior and on processes in human bodies and minds. Do we know the meaning and the timing of "Full," "New," "First Quarter," "Third Quarter," "Gibbous," "waxing" and "waning"? Randy did; and using his knowledge of the moon's influence in its various phases, he tried to schedule some of his outings close to the time of the full moon, when wolves howl and everyone's energy seems to skyrocket. Such a trip was his moonlight outing in the Harper Creek Wilderness. I enjoyed that trip so much that later I decided to lead others into the area by the light of the full moon.

Randy's idea was that participants in his outing needed to learn their way by moonlight. By turning off their flashlights or leaving them at home, they'd allow themselves the experience of finding their way by night — by choice — as our cave-dwelling ancestors no doubt did out of necessity. I am sure that Randy had his electric torch in reserve inside his pack in case the evening should be cloudy or some other emergency should arise. But he felt that it was a good idea for people first to attune themselves to the moon's rhythms and then learn to cope without artificial light in every phase of the moon.

I found myself in harmony with his philosophy and prepared to emulate his full-moon hiking plan. What could be more charming than a hike in the moonlight — especially when the base camp was a few miles from the trailhead and the trip from home, after work on a Friday, consumed several hours and the group arrived after dark? Necessity is sometimes the mother of intention.

I remember vividly the trip from trailhead to base camp in the moonlight. Other aspects of the trip are also memorable: our circuit hike to North Harper Creek and back to camp by way of Harper Creek Falls; our dips in pools along the way. In the July heat, those dips in cold mountain water were a comfort. What I recall most vividly of that trip, though, frankly, is the hike from base camp back to our vehicles at the close of the week-end. By this time I'd gotten somewhat acquainted with a young woman whom I'd met for the first time on that hike. I'll call her Belinda.

Belinda has made a big impression on me. She is a tall, slender brunette who wears glasses. But it isn't her appearance that impresses me; it is her camping style. Belinda's camp is as much like a well-appointed penthouse as any campsite I've ever seen. Beginning with the tent, the hammock, the camp stool, cooking equipment and library of the latest issues of several magazines, it goes on to include many small items of toiletry not ever seen in my *house*, much less my *campsite*. I find it hard to imagine how she has managed to carry them in from the trailhead, a distance of perhaps four or five miles. But I wasn't observing her in the moon's half-light.

When we hike out late Sunday afternoon, I can see better. And having marveled at her outdoor establishment, with nearly all the comforts of home except the kitchen sink, I can't wait to see how the moving van she has carried on her back will negotiate the narrow trails.

Evidently, however, she has mastered the art of loading her frame back-pack and of tying on each excess item to the outside of it.

I am also curious about the weight of her pack. My curiosity is soon satisfied.

"Can someone help me on with this pack?" she says to no one in particular.

Rashly, I volunteer. It's no big deal. People are always helping others on or off with their packs.

"Holy smoke! I'll bet this pack weighs eighty-five pounds!"

"D'ya think? What does yours weigh?"

"About twenty-five. You know what the sage preached: 'A man is rich in proportion to the number of things he can do without.' "

Our little group of nine persons forms a single file, Randy at the head, I taking up the rear, and marches along the creek to the crossing of its tributary, turns right and proceeds up a slight grade and then down another slight grade. Soon, though, comes the challenge: a long climb to the saddle. Seven persons' backs recede from view, and Belinda and I are the lone stragglers. I am committed to "bring up the rear," and Belinda is it, her steps growing more and more labored and slow as the others disappear. Halfway up the long incline, Randy and the others are waiting for us.

"Having trouble?" Randy asks pleasantly.

Belinda: "I think I packed too much."

I make a rash offer. "Do you want to swap?"

"Well — "

"Try it." I drop my rucksack and start to help her off with her huge pack. She hesitates and looks at Randy.

"He's strong," Randy says, taking off Belinda's pack and helping me strap it on.

Even with the lighter pack, Belinda struggles up the mountain; the others outdistance us again.

I have no wish to shoulder another eighty-five-pound back-pack. Do you suppose it was because of the full moon that a sixty-year-old guy would (and could) carry a pack for an overzealous and under-muscled thirty-year-old?

❖

Once I'd experienced Randy's moonlight hikes, I had to try to lead one myself; and once I'd done that, I was hooked. For a long time I scheduled most of my trips at the time of the full moon. I knew from reading that wolves and other animals howl and prowl in this phase of the moon. Then I learned from experience that when the moon was full, my cup of energy threatened to overflow.

I want to tell you about another moon-drenched week-end outing with the same locale and ground-rules: another base-camp trip in the Harper Creek wilderness.

❖

Deep in the woods, in summer, when the foliage is thick on the trees, moonlight scarcely reaches the ground to light the path. Thus the six or seven persons who meet at the trailhead at the appointed time are not content to settle for the moon's meager light. They insist on burning the EVEREADY™ batteries in their electric torches. Nevertheless, we have trouble staying on the trail. After the initial climb from the road, the trail descends to a flat creekside area where it is often obscured by low-growing, water-loving plants. Somehow we get through, climb to the saddle, make the long descent, climb the next rise and arrive at the campsite, where we set up by moonlight. The setting up is facilitated by two factors: (1) trees are sparse in the flat camping area near Harper Creek; and (2) by now the moon is high enough to be shining down more directly than in its first appearance above the horizon.

Unfortunately, not everyone on a Sierra Club outing conforms to the prescribed timetable. Someone in the group has given me a message from two men who plan to arrive late. I am to meet them not at the trailhead but at a grocery store several miles back. No one is in a position or condition to accompany me back to the trailhead; all are too tired or too busy. The doughty, intrepid leader is not allowed to be tired. Contenting myself with the thankless role of Responsible Trip Leader and armed with a description of the latecomers, I start the long up-and-down hike back to the trailhead, where I have parked my trusty old truck.

The moon, of course, is now higher and shines more directly down through the trees, losing less light than it would shining horizontally through the thickness of many trunks.

And fortunately, the place where the trail got lost on our way up (*I was never lost; no, sir!*) is in a relatively treeless and therefore relatively moonlit area. Incidentally, I am not carrying a flashlight. Foolhardy or *macho,* I am out to set some kind of example for the troops.

I find the trailhead.

I find the truck.

I find the grocery store.

I find the two latecomers.

We find the trailhead.

We park the vehicles, and my two fellow travelers strap on their packs. Now the fun starts.

The tougher-looking of the pair insists he wants to lead. I worry that he'll get us lost; I have visions of the three of us wandering all night in the flats looking for the path toward the long climb to the saddle.

Sure enough.

"Uh-oh," I soon hear Tough-Guy say.

"What's up?"

"Where does the trail go from here?"

You'd think, wouldn't you, that I'd have it memorized by this time; but it takes several minutes of thrashing about in the low shrubs before I find what I am pretty sure is the trail, going off in what I am pretty sure is the right direction (I am flying "blind"; that is, without map or compass). And after I have convinced myself that I am headed right, it takes a few minutes to persuade the others. You know how these things are; each guy wishes to be the *macho* hero who saves the group from danger and destruction. Finally, without saying anything at all, I assume the lead, and without saying anything at all, the others follow. I am getting tired, but do you think I'll say that out loud? I am pretty sure we'll have no more pathfinding problems.

The next day is what we live for: the circuit hike through the wilderness to North Harper Creek. We follow it to its confluence with Harper and then complete the circuit to the campsite. On this Circle Tour there are two highlights. One is the frequent dips in cool North Harper Creek. The other is the spectacular view from a cliff down toward North Harper, racing down over a steep rock-face.

I wonder if it would be more spectacular by moonlight. ❖

— ELEVEN - AFOOT —
Summer / Winter with the Outdoor Guru

— ELEVEN - AFOOT —
Summer / Winter with the Outdoor Guru

ADVENTURE SITE
Doughton Park, Blue Ridge Parkway • Uwharrie National Forest, North Carolina

You might be tempted to imagine Doughton Park, on the Blue Ridge Parkway, as tiny, trim and accessible.

That would be the wrong image.

In fact, it is remote and undeveloped — and extensive enough to be a good place to get lost — or to be trained in not getting lost. It is a good location for Randy's Sierra Club "Workshop" for potential outings leaders.

Randy was trained in the National Outdoor Leadership School and is a knowledgeable outdoor person. Furthermore, he has a quiet, unassuming style that doesn't turn off even those who already "know it all."

Randy's teaching begins when I call to sign up for his outing. Characteristically, his pedagogy takes the form of questions.

"What kind of tent do you have?"

"What kind of cooking equipment?"

"Sleeping equipment?"

"Rain gear?"

"Warm clothes?"

"First aid equipment?"

"How would you feel about sharing a tent with a perfect stranger?"

"Of the opposite gender?"

I try to answer as openly and honestly as I can.

"Are you prepared to car pool?"

"Well, sure. I'm a serious environmentalist."

"Are you prepared to help with simulations?"

"With what?"

"With role-playing situations that can occur in the woods?"

"Well, sure." I'm a teacher, and I've used role-playing, and I know how it works.

At the trailhead we count noses and tents. Since there are eight of us, Randy allows us four two-person tents. I am elected to leave mine behind. That's okay with me, for it's a leaky discount-store special, and frankly, a damned nuisance. I am also elected to team up with Barbara at bed time. I have to admit that this is quite a novel idea to me. I look at Barbara, a slightly overweight thirty-year-old nurse who is becoming interested in forest conservation issues and allows as how it's time for her to develop campcraft and other wilderness skills. She doesn't seem bothered at being the bed-mate of a middle-aged guy. She's bunked with several male buddies to whom she was not romantically attached.

We divide up gear. Barbara has a lot of cooking equipment; I carry the tent. Randy also divides up the food which he's purchased with our pooled money. I am given the heavy responsibility of carrying two big plastic tubs of peanut butter.

The hike in seems long but uneventful except for the damage, pointed out by Randy, to a couple of trees along the trail.

"Boy scouts," he says.

"Really?"

"I think so."

"How do you know?" someone asks.

"The scars weren't there when I scouted this trip two weeks ago. That same week-end there were some scouts camped over there beyond the ridge."

"Boy scouts and their little hatchets," someone remarks wryly.

It is dark when we arrive at the campsite. Setting up a tent in the dark is no challenge to an old wilderness hand, and following Barbara's lead, I have little trouble being helpful, though unfamiliar with her state-of-the-art backpacker's tent. Tent up, we toss our gear inside, including the two tubs of peanut butter. I debate putting them in a bag and running it up a line thrown over a high limb, but Randy is already calling the group together around — not a campfire — but his little hanging candle lantern; therefore I don't take the time. Hardly has the group gathered for Session Number One, on outdoor cookery, when I hear a familiar sound from "our" tent.

"Uh-oh!" says Barbara.

I run back to the tent to retrieve the peanut butter tubs. There is only one. A brief search does not turn up the missing tub.

"Lesson One," says Randy when I bring back *one* tub of peanut butter and the sad report. "Raccoons are cleverer than you think they are, and we should have hung up all the food not in metal. Do you know how to do it?"

All but one guy claim to know how, but each version of how to keep food away from wild animals is different from all the others.

"Whatever works," says Randy, and proceeds with his lesson on outdoor cooking. His stir-fried vegetable dinner is a great success.

With good will and good humor, going to bed with a platonic friend need be no trouble. Considerations of space in a two-person tent inevitably decree that one person dress for bed and crawl into the sleeping bag before the other person enters the tent. We don't talk much, except about that cussed clever raccoon. We're tired.

In the morning we find the missing peanut butter tub a few yards from the tent. Now it's half empty.

Randy is a good teacher; he's planned well. After breakfast on Sunday we hike cross-country, using map and compass to arrive at a "saddle," Randy's favorite topographic feature. On the way he has us fan out instead of playing "Follow the Leader" in order, he says, to prevent starting new, impromptu paths through previously pathless wilderness. From the saddle we continue climbing on our "round trip" back to camp. During the trip we do our "simulations." Randy approaches one or two of us at a time as we hike in our "fanned-out" non-formation, assigning each a role in a wilderness mini-drama. He casts me as a mean old snake-killer, and on cue I pick up a thick piece of tree-limb and begin beating on an imaginary snake.

"What are you doing?" Barbara cries, running up to me at the risk of life and limb. Randy has evidently cast her as a snake-lover.

"I'm killing this wicked snake."

"Why?"

"I hate snakes."

"What did they ever do to you?"

"They was born."

"But they were here first. This is their turf. We're just guests here."

"Well, he could bite me, and he might be poisonous."

"This one's not poisonous. You can tell by the shape of his head."

"But he could still bite."

"Not really. Snakes usually run away when they hear someone coming."

"Well —"

"Maybe if you're afraid of snakes you'd feel better staying in the house."

"I'm afraid of 'em in there, too."

"But there you'd have a better right to attack them."

By this time all the other trainees are gathered around and are getting the point.

Randy casts me in another role as we climb a rather steep ridge through open climax forest. This time I am an old codger having a heart attack. The situation is realistic, for I am, in fact, the oldest member of the group, and I am getting winded from the climb. I do not, of course, see myself as a candidate for a heart attack, for as an active runner I'm in fair cardiovascular condition; but I go along with Randy's educational program.

I pick a comfortable-looking bed of leaves and fall down gasping and panting. "Oh! Oh! Oh!"

Jack comes running over. "What's the matter?"

"I can't breathe."

"Here; let me lift your head a bit." He kneels, raising my head and resting it on his knee. "Someone wet a handkerchief," he says, as others come running up. Barbara takes off her bandanna and pours water on it from her canteen.

"Oh! I think I'm dying." Actually, I am rather enjoying all this attention.

We abandon the exercise after everyone has a chance to watch the ham actor hamming the symptoms and to observe the others applying first aid.

We continue upward toward the top of the ridge.

Dan stops in his tracks and puts his hand to his ear. He seems to be hearing distant thunder.

"Listen up, everybody! There's a storm coming — pretty fast. We need to get off this ridge. Here we're exposed to a lightning strike. And let's get out from under these tall trees. I think there's a cave up here. Maybe it's big enough for all of us."

We are learning to cope in the wilderness. ❖

FREEZING IN UWHARRIE — PRELUDE

Why do we not venture into the wilderness in "inclement weather"?
Because we fear becoming cold and wet.
But what if there is a science of dealing with inclement weather?
All weather, say the Chinese, is of the gods; therefore how can any weather be "bad"? But listen to the weather reports on radio or television; how many reporters insist on making value judgments?
"It's going to be a good week-end."
"Bad weather on the way, folks."
It's one thing to issue freeze warnings, tornado watches, hurricane and small-craft advisories and flood watches; but it's another to say, "This weather is *bad*; that weather is *good*." All weather simply IS. Weather is the GREAT I-AM.

❖

Two experiences in the Uwharrie illustrate how proper preparation for inclement weather can remove one's fear of it. In the first I am unprepared because I do not have the benefit of good advice and good preparation. In the second, I am under the tutelage of Randy the Outdoor Guru.

❖

What is the proper garb for an early fall service outing in the Uwharrie? Tough blue jeans; right? Not necessarily. It depends on the weather.

❖

We are to relocate an overused trail in the Uwharrie National Forest. This particular national forest consists of overworked farmland which was bought by the Federal Government and allowed to return to its natural state.
Our group of a dozen volunteers is divided into two crews, with two different tasks. We arrive at mid-morning; work; eat lunch; work some more. Then we are to meet back at the trailhead before dark for the homeward car-pool.
Have I listened to the weather forecast? No. Am I prepared? Not really.
It rains lightly but steadily from noon until mid-afternoon. Am I wearing thermal underwear? No. Rain gear? No. Before long, from the rain directly and from the thrashing of wet brush against my clothes, my heavy Levis® are thoroughly soaked. When cotton gets wet, it stays wet a long time. And if the day is cold, the cotton gets cold. *And* stays cold against my skin, which enjoys being warm.

My crew finishes early and has a long wait at the trailhead. Sitting indoors is not an option, and the vehicles are locked. The best I can do is walk about and try to stimulate blood circulation to generate body heat. Nevertheless, I do a lot of shivering before the others show up and I have access to a blessed car heater. A change into dry clothes would be wonderfully comforting. Advice about clothing before the fact would have been even more valuable: (BRING RAIN-GEAR; WEAR WOOL AND/OR SYNTHETICS; DRESS IN WATER-SHEDDING OR WARM-WHEN-WET CLOTHES).

I paid dearly in discomfort for that FOREST SERVICE VOLUNTEER patch.

WINTER TRAINING IN THE UWHARRIE NATIONAL FOREST

Randy's "Winter Camping Workshop" resembles desensitization therapy, in which the therapist encourages the client to confront the phobia directly while the professional stands by to offer advice and support. The fear in question is the fear of freezing in the woods. The workshop is held in December.

Planning an outdoor experience in December is a lot like rolling the dice. Several outcomes are possible. They may be limited in number, but the outcome is always in doubt. It's a brave group of nine persons who sign up for Randy's outing and then *actually show up!*

We are to back-pack into the interior of the Birkhead Mountain section. Randy, in publicizing the workshop, warns us to prepare for a wide range of possible weather conditions. If anyone in the group has failed to do so, I do not hear about it.

On the days preceding the outing, the weather pattern is one of increasing cold. We've had several days of frost, not an unusual phenomenon for this time of year. We have been warned to prepare for: (1) rain; (2) snow; (3) freezing temperatures, or, conversely, (4) warm weather or (5) any combination of these. When we leave home for the Uwharrie, the weather is cloudy and cool: a fairly typical winter day. It looks and feels stormy. One's inner barometer warns of heavy weather on the way.

According to his philosophy of minimum impact on the wilderness, Randy has us carry in the smallest feasible number of tents and a minimum of other gear. It is cool as we leave the trailhead, well below 40° and seemingly getting colder. As we make last-minute adjustments to our gear before slinging our packs on our backs, Randy circulates asking questions. He doesn't inspect packs or give advice; that isn't his style, but it is always clear what he thinks ought to be included and what left out of our packs for maximum preparedness and minimum impact. Since food preparation is to be on an individual basis, each person is encouraged to take plenty of food to fortify against the anticipated cold. Tent sharing is recommended, but I am "odd man out," without a tent mate. Therefore I carry my little orange-and-blue nylon pup-tent, along with a huge nylon tarp to fly over it — hardly state-of-the-art, but the best I own.

We've hiked two miles when light rain begins falling. Fortunately, the drops don't freeze on the ground; that would create hazardous conditions underfoot. We stop and don our rain gear. With rain increasing, we stride briskly single file along the narrow trail, not really worried about the drip and splash from tall grass and tree limbs. Yes; since we are adequately attired and properly "desensitized," we even enjoy trekking the last two miles to the campsite.

The site is an established one in a circular basin surrounded by a climax forest. It has been provided with a stone fireplace, probably built by boy scouts. After a hand-freezing lunch around the fire, we set out for an afternoon hike. Randy has planned carefully, for as we file, mostly on trails, we encounter several fire rings, large stones arranged in circles. These we eradicate by tossing the stones into the woods in all directions, scattering the remaining charred wood and placing a "natural" cover of leaves on the afflicted areas. From previous experience on Randy's hikes I am aware that he holds the "new" wilderness ethic which rules out campfires merely for aesthetic or social reasons and advocates fire for emergency situations only. I agree that to encounter rings of blackened stones every few rods along the trail offends the aesthetic sense and diminishes the feeling of being out where few but four-footed creatures ever go.

Especially offensive is the stone fireplace — *held together with cement mortar* — which we find near the trail and proceed to demolish. This in a national forest! What could the scouts have in mind in creating such a permanent structure in a dedicated wilderness area? I find myself hoping that the instructions I've seen in scout manuals when I was a boy have now been dropped: how to build pot-hangers, outdoor furniture and the like, using knife and hatchet.

After this ostensibly instructive activity, of which I feel sure Mother Nature approves, we prepare another hand-freezing meal around the fire at camp, during which the light fades. We haven't seen the sun all day, but it must have been there; and when it departs, we miss it. After only a brief social and instructional session, it is dark, and we are ready to retire.

I have asked Randy to inspect the big nylon tarp which I routinely rig over my tent to keep off rain and snow. I depend on long ropes tied to four trees and the four corners of the tarp; and it isn't easy to hang the tarp so that it will shed rain efficiently. There is always some tendency, especially if one doesn't stretch the ropes tightly enough, for the tarp to sag somewhere, creating a pool which will leak eventually, dripping water onto the nylon tent. Then, if I touch the inside of the wet tent, that spot will drip water, wetting my sleeping bag and me. I definitely don't want that to happen on a night when any water within reach will likely be ice before morning.

"Looks okay to me," Randy comments, after walking around to inspect my rig.

"Bring a bar of chocolate," Randy had suggested. "Take it into the tent with you. If you wake up cold, break off a piece and eat it."

I have followed his suggestion with a vengeance, placing one of those huge eight-ounce bars of pure chocolate under my pillow. In fact, so sure am I that I'll need the warmth that I start the campaign before retiring and, because I wake up shivering several times during the night, the entire half-pound bar is gone by morning. It is cold when I awake in the morning light. There is ice on the ground and ice on the tarp. But my tent is dry, and so am I.

At breakfast, when all of us are standing around in the common area near the fire, Randy announces that he's placed two thermometers during the night. Outside his tent, he says, the temperature was 22° Fahrenheit. Inside, it was 26°. Brr-rr-rr!

Standing about in the morning, before we've done much to get our circulation going, we have some trouble keeping our hands and feet warm.

"Swing your arms." Randy suggests. "Then hold onto a tree and swing your legs." With a twinkle he adds, "One at a time."

After breakfast, each camper packs a lunch, straps on a water bottle and prepares for another hike — this time cross-country. We are out, I tell myself, for a pleasant rustling and crunching over ice-covered leaves. And so it proves. But the didactic element is not lacking. As we leave the circle of five widely placed tents and climb the hill from the sheltered basin, Randy leads us through a hillside area where, he says, soldiers on a training maneuver from nearby

Fort Bragg have bivouacked. A little investigation would have led even a casual observer to that conclusion. The ground is littered with C-ration cans and candy wrappers.

No rain falls on Sunday, and by mid-afternoon, when we return to strike camp, it is warm enough to have melted the ice and even partly dried my tent and tarp. We pack up and hike out under a light overcast. I hear no one complaining. No one is suffering. No one, it appears, is wet or cold.

◆

We have benefited from the wisdom of the Outdoor Guru. ❖

—TWELVE - AFOOT—
LISTENING TO CHRIS

—TWELVE - AFOOT—
LISTENING TO CHRIS

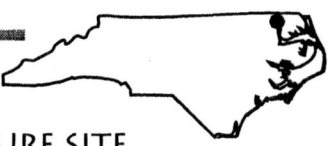

ADVENTURE SITE
*Merchants Millpond State Park
North Carolina*

I'm a strong advocate of studying nature's ways and acting in accordance with natural law. To me, there's no substitute for direct experience, in spite of Dave Christie.

Dave was my classmate in high school. I'll never forget the time when he was a kind gentleman and held the handle of the water fountain for me. It was one of those that would shoot higher and higher the farther you turned the handle. Dave started by producing a gentle, manageable flow of water — until I got my face well into the process. Then he unleashed a faceful.

"Experience is a dear teacher," he intoned, "but fools may profit by no other."

I agree that first-hand experience is superior to the second- or third-hand stuff Dave and I were getting from our textbooks and teachers. Dave's squirt in the eye was a splash of direct experience, and I've never forgotten it. But there are other teachers. Intuition, for example.

It's ideal when long association breeds familiarity. I have lived at my house long enough to be able to find my way through it in total darkness with hardly a stubbed toe. There are also places in the natural world where I am almost as much "at home" as that. Such a place is the trail system at Merchants Millpond State Park. But I submit that I was not wrong to suppress my knowledge at a fork in the trail one dark midnight in the interests of a higher *human* good. I'll tell the tale and let you judge.

❖

When I first moved to my remote homestead in a rural county, the enterprising director of the county's Youth Services Bureau recruited me to be on the Board of Directors. One of the hardest programs to operate was the one patterned after Big Brothers / Big Sisters. There were never enough adults to match the large number of boys and girls who were in trouble with the school, or the law, or their neighbors, or their parents. And so I volunteered and was matched with Chris, a slight 13-year-old who had a deep distrust of all adult males, having been deserted by his father and abused by a succession of stepfather and "mama's boy-friend" types.

My panacea is the outdoor life. My school is nature. I tend to think: "If in doubt, get on out," out into the sweet-smelling natural world, and inhale its influence. And so Chris, in a succession of week-end outings, accompanied me to a lot of my favorite places. One of these was Merchants Millpond State Park.

◆

We do not go directly to the Park. We spend part of the first day of our week-end exploring Lake Drummond, in the heart of the Great Dismal Swamp. To get there we have to paddle upstream from the "feeder" canal that parallels U.S. Highway 17.

Actually, the "feeder" canal was built not to "feed" but to drain Lake Drummond. The water level in Lake Drummond is controlled by a dam, and the water flowing over the dam rushes downstream to the "feeder" through a narrow channel.

If George Washington had been a better or a more persistent engineer, there would not remain even the tiny portion we now see of the far greater Great Dismal Swamp, which he proposed to drain, log, and farm. Fortunately, the scheme fell short of demolishing the Great Dismal completely.

Paddling upstream is not my favorite activity. I'll do it if I have to. If I want to get to Lake Drummond by canoe, I have to. After looking at a couple of points on the "feeder" canal, Chris and I dismount from the Chevy pick-up, unload the boat and put in. From the first stroke of our paddles, we are contending with stiff current.

Chris performs pretty well. He doesn't have a lot of power, nor a lot of energy, nor much more than a trace of resolve, but he sits in the bow and responds to my urgings by continuing to dip the paddle and do his share. We continue for half an hour pulling the smooth-bottomed whitewater boat up through the strong current.

"Paddle, Chris!"

And finally, the dam comes into view, with its gently graded spillway off to the side, a defunct conveyer at its head for hauling boats up the last short incline to lake level. Here we launch again in a narrow canal that leads out to the broad, flat and eerie plain of Lake Drummond.

Really, once there, we find the place to be a bit of a disappointment. Unique, yes; but little more, really, than a huge lake ringed with wet shores where stunted trees are draped with Spanish moss. Here and there a dead-looking hulk of cypress thrusts its knees and the rest of its anatomy out of the shallow flatness of black water. We do not stay long.

Never mind. Lake Drummond is not the be-all and end-all. Our major destination for the week-end is Merchants Millpond State Park. It is also our intended bivouac for the night. At the edge of the pond, near the park office, we take our camping gear from the truck and load it into the boat. We follow the line of faded green buoys that leads to the family campground. We pick a site and set up camp. After a quick, cold supper (I'm too lazy to cook in the outdoors), we set out to hunt beavers.

Beavers are nocturnal. That's why they're rarely seen unless one goes out by dawn's early light or at dusk, when the light is fading. Chris sits in the bow, holding the light, his security blanket. Like all kids, he loves flashlights. I am apprehensive as we leave the line of buoys that leads to the center of the pond. I know that the beaver lodges are to the left, in "no man's land" where there are no guiding plastic floats; and I know that moss-draped cypress and tupelo trees tend to look very much alike. I am aware that it is very easy to get lost on this pond.

The worst of it is that though we do see one set of eyes moving smoothly on the pond's surface, it quickly becomes too dark to see much of anything except when Chris turns on my big searchlight; and of course the beam of the light illuminates but a tiny portion of the round horizon's 360 degrees. In short, we quickly become disoriented.

Well, there's a better word for it.

Lost.

Lost on the pond.

Now the emphasis changes in a hurry. Our aim was to satisfy our curiosity about beavers. Our aim now is survival.

We probably wander for an hour, I turning the boat in response to what at first I pretend are rational considerations. We look for evidence of sunset afterglow in the west (not that that will help much in this crescent-shaped pond dotted with trees and hummocks that break up any line one might draw from one point to another). But try as we may, we can't find another of those guiding light-green buoys or any sign of the sunset glow. Even if the clouds were not swallowing the starlight, the heavy tree canopy would.

Chris is clearly frightened but gamely refraining from becoming hysterical. Now I am acting out of something even less tangible than intuition. Call it survival instinct. Unable to see any sign of civilization, here represented directly by the buoys that would lead us back to our campsite, I am eager to respond to anything resembling a signpost or landmark. Anxiously scanning the horizon, I detect a light. Is it moving? Evidently not. Therefore it must be shore-based.

I am now ready to head for any reliable reference point or, failing that, any mere sign of civilization that will lead us, if not back to the camp, then to some other place where we can get some much-needed rest. We have been driving, paddling, setting up tent and exerting in other ways all day this Saturday and are ready for some "Z's." As for Chris, he is far from having any clear ideas about what to do and is in a mode of trusting my presumably superior experience — for now. And so, when I spy a light, we head for it; and when the boat, threading between trees rooted in the shallows, strikes a solid shore, we beach on it and take off cross country toward the greatest number of visible lights.

Crossing a field, we come to a paved public road that I suspect is County Road 1400 which, connecting US 158 and NC 37, crosses Lassiter Creek in passing the park. Indeed, that's what it proves to be, and after walking, we come to the park entrance.

Why do we now not retrace our steps to the boat, haul it out and paddle the line of buoys to the campsite?

Good question.

Answer: having just traversed unfamiliar terrain — in the dark — I am not at all sure I can retrace my steps and find the boat. And if we could find it, we'd have to drag it a mile or so through cypress and across a field, not a pleasant prospect. Actually, I give these considerations hardly a moment's thought, for I know a way back to the campsite — on trails (mostly).

Forward! We cross the bridge over Lassiter Creek.

Now I have been here several times before and know the place. I know, too, that several steps beyond, we will be able to step to the right, away from the road, and take a trail which circles the northern half of the pond. Following it, we'll skirt the pond; at a certain point (not so easy to identify in this almost total darkness) strike off to the right through the woods and arrive at the campground. I describe all this to Chris, who seems to be neither comforted nor convinced. Nevertheless, we set off down the trail. I am familiar enough with this trail to feel at home on it and even anticipate some of its twistings and turnings.

We come to a "Y."

Now I must tell you that this "Y" and the choice which it presents is the climax of the story; the rest is anti-climax.

You may not believe what happens next. I can hardly believe it myself; nevertheless, I think I can rationalize my irrational behavior at this point.

Here's what unexpected, inexplicable thing happens.

I say, "Chris, the right-hand trail goes around the pond and will take us back to our campsite. The left-hand leads — after several miles — to one park entrance, not the main one, but the one on U.S. 158. It also leads to the backpacking camp. We want to take the right-hand trail."

Chris looks at me. It is dark, but he has the flashlight. I am sure he needs it for comfort and cheer. I know he is tired from paddling. I suspect that in his weariness he is reverting to his long-standing and deeply-held suspicion of <u>all adult males</u>. But I never suspect that these considerations will lead him to be totally irrational.

"No," he says. "I think we should take the left-hand trail."

Is it because the left one leads downhill?

"Chris, I've been here several times before. I know for a fact that the right-hand trail leads us back to our tent."

"No; let's go this way."

Chris is wearing tennis shoes, not the best footgear for hiking. I am wearing my neoprene river boots, likewise not the best footgear for walking. I am not a bit eager to take a midnight hike — in the wrong direction — wearing boots, still full of water from stepping out of and beaching the boat — with a kid who is not far from wearing down completely. But I can tell he is not to be moved from his totally wrong-headed conclusion about which is the right path.

We turn left.

We hike a mile and a half. We come to the old road and turn left. We arrive at U.S. 158. We turn left on it and arrive at the park entrance. Chris is finally persuaded that I have been telling him the truth.

But so what? We are now 'way out in left field without a fielder's glove. What to do? We are into the wee small hours of Sunday morning so far as our metabolism is concerned. We have been awake since early morning: driving, paddling, being lost, hiking. We are tired. We need sleep. Especially, Chris needs sleep. But we are not going to be able to find a sleeping place that Chris will consider satisfactory without considerable more *schlepping*.

Evidently Chris has now reached the end of his determined resistance to adult male authority, and it is again up to me to determine a course of action. I propose that we hike back to the *other* park entrance, where my truck is parked, that we get into it and drive to the nearest motel (Elizabeth City, nearly thirty miles from the park) and crash.

✧

If I'd been alone, I'd have had a better, cheaper night's sleep in the tent. Chris' presence made the whole experience considerably more complicated and expensive.

Now I put it to you: what would you have done?

Would you have followed what you *knew* from experience and pulled your adult male rank?

Or would you have employed your third ear in listening to Chris? ❖

—THIRTEEN - AFOOT—
Climbing Ktaadn

—THIRTEEN - AFOOT—
Climbing Ktaadn

ADVENTURE SITE
*Baxter State Park
Maine*

You will note that in naming the mountain I follow the orthography of one of my heroes, Henry David Thoreau, who made at least three visits to Maine, climbed the mountain at least once and published "Ktaadn and the Maine Woods" in *Union Magazine* in 1848.

The northern terminus of the Applachian Trail is located at the summit of Mt. Ktaadn.

I've never tried through-hiking the Appalachian Trail. I've traveled only a couple of sections. One of these I tell about in **Trip Six - Afoot — Brown Bears and Blueberries.** Maybe some day I'll attempt the entire trail, but I don't think so. You'll know why when I describe the last few miles of the Trail. I should say that in the tale related here I describe not the *very* last miles; I couldn't do that because I never got to the top. I am writing to provide information for anyone considering a through-hike on the AT.

In order to make a continuous trek from south to north on the AT, a hiker has to start from Springer Mountain, in Georgia, so early in spring that there will likely still be snow on the ground. Even at a moderate pace she or he will hardly arrive at Ktaadn summit before the snow begins falling again in Maine. And I do not believe you will wish to be hiking the last bit of trail on Mt. Ktaadn when the snow is falling. You'll see why.

Mt. Ktaadn (the name is an Indian one, like many names of Maine's natural features) is located in Baxter State Park, the most beautiful state park I have ever visited. The tale of the Maine governor who donated his vast estate to preserve it in perpetuity for the state's citizens makes a fine story in itself, but you'll have to read it somewhere else. And not only is Baxter a wonderfully scenic place, a place of lakes with Indian names, of clear, cold streams where browsing moose may or may not move out of your way when you float up to them in your canoe or even if you point your car at them on the road. Baxter is the best-kept state park I know and has the most environmentally determined and consistent policies you'll find anywhere. Would you believe me if I told you that there are no trash receptacles in the park? You are expected to take out whatever you bring in, with the exception of what you deposit in the privy.

❖

The lean-to where Lea and I camp has its back to the dirt track that runs through the campground. Its face is toward Nesowadnehunk Stream, which at this place is a brook not over fifteen feet wide making bubbles in its leaps over soft-ball-sized stream "pebbles," lulling us with its peaceful murmuring. From here we make forays in the canoe, in the car and on foot. On one of them we float upstream toward Nesowadnehunk Lake, encountering a browsing young moose. But our major adventure is the climb on Ktaadn.

There are at least three dozen trails we can take, and most of them climb high or low mountains. But why settle for less than the supreme endeavor?

Ideally the Ktaadn climber tackles the mountain in stages, camping at Roaring Brook Campground, which is closer to the summit, or at Chimney Pond Campground, which is partway up the mountain. But permits are required for any campground in the park; preference is given to residents of Maine; permits take considerable exchange of correspondence and lapse of time; and one takes what one can get.

The distance from our trailhead, "Katahdin Stream Campground," to the summit via the "Hunt Trail" is a mere 5.19 miles, but considering the height of the mountain (its top 5,267 feet above the sea), and taken with the change of elevation from the stream to the summit, it is "a good day's trip" up and back. I have a hard time contemplating such an ending to a hike of 3,298 kilometers; that is, 2050 miles, on the Appalachian Trail, the world's longest continuous mountain trail.

It is Friday, July 26, 1991. Tonight we shall see a full moon. This morning, at 7:30, we should be full of energy as we park the car at "Katahdin Stream Campground" and take to the trail. We pass tents from which campers are just emerging to pursue their morning ablutions. In minutes we are in the woods, walking briskly along a broad trail flanked by tall trees. The gradient of the trail increases gradually, but we, fresh from rest and eager to reach the top, stride along with confidence and energy, side by side. Surprisingly, we encounter other hikers, one after the other, meeting us on their way down the mountain. How early must all of these eager hikers have started from the summit? In fact, we meet one man in shorts, neckerchief and Tyrolean hat who has already this morning climbed from Chimney Pond, on the other side of the mountain, to the summit, and is now on his way down.

When the trail narrows to single-file width, I let Lea go ahead. She sets a slower pace than I might do. I have little talent for pacing myself; I tend to keep putting out effort until there's no more energy left; then I collapse.

By noon we are doing more knee-lifting than mere thrusting of the feet forward. Every few yards the next forward step is like a stair step, a foot of riser and the next tread a flat rock. We are walking more on paint-blazed rocks than on leaf-covered soil, and when we perch on a trailside rock to eat our lunch, we can look not only down on Dacey Pond but also to our right (north), where even the summit of "The Owl" (3,715' above sea level) seems no higher than our vantage point.

We are soon above the tree line. Looking up, we are surprised and dismayed to see little except huge boulders, with less and less walking space and more places where continuing to advance means searching for cairns or paint blazes on bare rock. To see the trail ahead, we must tilt our heads back sharply, with resulting pain in the neck and distress to the "onward" spirit. It is a sunny and only slightly breezy day, but we can imagine what it would be like to travel this mountain's flying buttress on a colder, windier day; we would be in danger of being swept off the spur which carries this rocky trail upward seemingly *ad infinitum*.

We cannot see the top. We see only boulders, rocks and more rocks and boulders, with paint marks on the more permanent-looking ones and occasional small rock-piles to mark the "trail." And more and more as we labor up this bald promontory we are aware of other human beings, most of them younger and speedier climbers, scrambling downward toward us from the top — when will we ever reach it? — entering our vision as tiny red or yellow or brown specks moving barely perceptively and gradually taking the shape of human beings with legs and swinging arms, moving with more energy than we can now imagine, as ours seems to ebb and desert us. The top looks impossible to achieve. But we plod on.

She does not say so, but I seem to notice that Lea is tiring.

Far below us, but close enough for identification and within hearing as they converse animatedly — how can they have breath enough both to climb and to talk? — a group of four young men is rapidly overtaking us as we confront an interesting challenge. The trail seems to stop at a vertical wall eight feet high and so broad as to block movement to either right or left — or up. But there is no other way to proceed <u>but</u> up, over the flat top of it to the next paint blaze.

Ah! On closer inspection we discover that someone has imbedded in the face of the rock a steel handhold which no doubt was intended as an aid to climbing. Unfortunately, the handhold has been broken or cut, and all that remains is a rounded stub of steel a couple of inches long protruding from the rock — not remotely adequate as a handhold or foot support.

As we stand there speculating, the four young fellows approach. It is evident that three of them are seasoned hikers about twenty years old; the fourth, a young boy of perhaps fifteen, makes no *macho* pretensions.

"Uh-oh!" says the boy.

"Hey! Not to worry," says one of the others. "You can handle it."

❖

Another of the three, looking at Lea and me, says "Maybe we should help these folks first."

"Great !" I say. "I'm not proud. I need all the help I can get."

Two of the young men stand against the rock making a footplace of their four hands. Without hesitation I step into it, using their shoulders to steady myself briefly, reach up to the top of the rock, take hold and thrust the other leg up. I stand and reach a hand to Lea as the young men boost from below. Before we leave the place, the three young men have helped their younger companion up and are showing us their backs as they proceed on their way, chatting merrily.

Lea and I are climbing now with diminished enthusiasm after this demonstration of our borderline decrepitude and ineptness for this kind of hiking. I can't help recalling the blind man who hiked the entire Appalachian Trail, accompanied for most of the way by only his seeing-eye dog and one other human companion. The article I read reported that he had fallen "*only __ times*" (I forget the number, but it was at least a couple of dozens). Such courage! And how would he have fared at this particular place? Maybe the handhold was still intact when he made his through-hike.

We are now struggling with both physical exhaustion and our disheartenment at failing to maintain that priceless image of invincibility. After gaining a few more yards of altitude; and in consideration of the seeming endlessness of this rocky spur; the additional hike on top to arrive at "Thoreau's Spring"; the length of the return trip; the condition of our already jellified knees and their need to supply braking power for a controlled descent — we determine that living to fight another day is more important than winning today.

Really, we make this determination mostly for Lea's benefit, since she is the one inclined to make a realistic assessment of her capabilities. As I said, I'm the one who uses up everything, and then tries to run on "Empty." In fact, in order to remove any onus from Lea for the decision to give up, I stop during our descent and pretend to collapse and take a nap on the trail.

The car seat has never felt so good.

Somewhat revived by an interlude in the car, we stop at a particularly inviting roadside pool in Nesowadnehunk Stream and take a dip. The air is still hot at five o'clock in the afternoon, and the stream eminently wadable: shallow water over table-like flat rocks, but so cold that total immersion is no temptation. We hardly even feel like using the cold water to erase the day's perspiration. ❖

ARMS PULLING — BACK BENDING

13 TALES AFLOAT

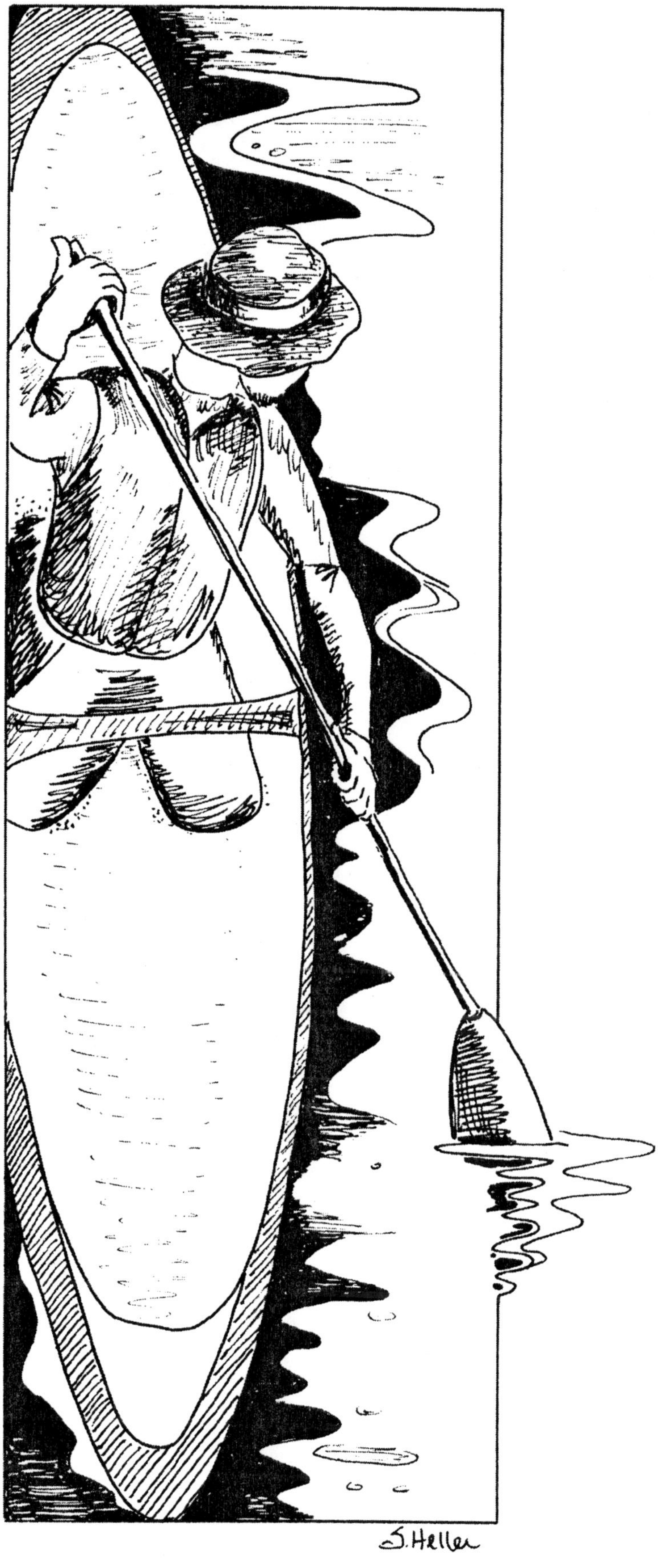

— ONE - AFLOAT —
Green on the New

— ONE - AFLOAT —
Green on the New

ADVENTURE SITE
*The New River, Ashe County
North Carolina*

Carol, whom you met in **Trip Eight - Afoot**, was the leader of my first river trip. I was definitely a green paddler. Because some of the other participants were as green as I was, Carol chose an easy section of the river, one appropriate for beginners. We paddled on the New River, said to be the oldest river in the United States and the second oldest on the planet.

I was a rank beginner, despite a brief exposure to the Boy Scouts when I was twelve. I hope our scout troop was unique. I remember only two kinds of activity from those days: the obscene initiation into the troop (you don't want to hear about it) and the experience, unique in my adolescence, of putting on the boxing gloves with my high school buddy Dave Christie. I recall no outdoor activity whatsoever with my old scout troop: no idyllic camporee, no lakeside instruction in canoe technique, not even any nautical study of knots, something that would have been a handy adjunct to outdoor life. I recall studying diagrams of knot-tying in the official scout handbook, but I was never introduced to boats as a scout.

I had never, for example, given any thought at all to the "trim" of a canoe; therefore I had no clue to the importance of lining up a partner whose weight would help "dress" the boat. Nor did anyone in the outing group suggest reversing the boat in the water for solo paddling, heading the stern downstream, and kneeling in the bilge with rump resting against the bow seat. Doing this would have placed my weight more nearly in the center of the boat's length, keeping the boat nearly level and easier to both balance and maneuver.

❖

I am to paddle solo in a rented tandem canoe. At the put-in, I hardly notice the nature of the broad, shallow river; I am filled with apprehension concerning this, my first-ever river trip. I have rented a life jacket along with the boat, but wearing it does not make me feel safe. I watch the others mount. I follow their example with what I trust looks like more confidence than I feel. Awkwardly I try to get the boat launched without wetting my feet.

This proves impossible; the water is shallow for some yards before it is deep enough to float the boat, though the other boats, with two occupants apiece, appear to draw but three inches of water. Finally, my hiking boots soaked (the wrong footgear for this sport), I find myself on the stern seat, feeling proud even to be able to identify bow and stern.

With all my weight in the stern, the bow and most of the rest of the boat rise out of the water, negating the stabilizing effect of the broad flat beam at the boat's center. My weight, and the weight of the boat's entire length (except for the narrow stern seat) float poised in the air, ready to overturn in any direction should an unconscious motion of mine tilt the craft even slightly.

Naturally, then, I haven't gone a kilometer before some unknowing movement of mine causes the boat to capsize, dumping me into the river. I have no idea what I did "wrong"; probably I leaned just a bit to one side or the other; it wouldn't take much to upset a boat which is hardly in the water at all.

Over goes the boat, with me in it. "Splash !" Somewhat to my surprise, I don't plunge into a great depth of water; there isn't enough water to sink in. My spine hits the sandy bottom almost before I realize I am out of the boat. So much for my fear of drowning in the New River.

Carol has been paddling with Danny, she in the bow, he in the stern. Seeing my predicament and evidently realizing that I haven't a clue how to cope, they paddle over. When I realize that I can stand up, I do so, watching as Carol and Danny empty the water and right my rented boat. Danny makes a suggestion.

"Why don't you reverse the boat? Point the stern downstream and sit on the bow seat; it'll put you closer to the center, and the boat will float more level." This is a novel idea to me; I feel quite certain that the bow is always the bow and that the rules decree that it must always be pointed downstream. Nevertheless, Danny sounds sincere and knowledgeable, and I trust him intuitively. He even holds the boat steady while I remount.

But I am having serious misgivings about the entire enterprise. Why did I think I'd enjoy learning to paddle a canoe? Why did I allow myself to be seduced into a trip on the famous New River? And especially, why did I think I could handle a canoe all by myself when I'd had no instruction and had no one to help? I could see myself struggling all week-end to keep the boat upright and, at the same time, paddle with enough confidence and energy to stay with the group.

Without saying all of this, I look at Carol, wishing she'd find one skilled and stalwart volunteer to take over my solo boat and another skilled paddler to take me in and give me some pointers.

The other half-dozen members of the flotilla, all of them paddling tandem, have come to my rescue, wading in the shallow river. Now they stand by giving me instruction, much of it going in one ear and out the other.. There's only so much that a person's mind can absorb when it's already clouded with embarrassment, apprehension and envy of anyone with skill and a partner.

After this rescue and some rudimentary instruction, I continue trying, with difficulty, to keep up with the group, all of whom but me have the advantage of tandem (two-person) paddle-power. Many are my under-the-breath expressions of anxiety and frustration.

With what little attention isn't focused on pure survival, I now notice that Carol and Danny make a pretty good team. But Carol, though competent, is not nearly so skillful as Danny. I do not know what is going on in Carol's head; I only know what considerations *ought* to be revolving in the mind and conscience of a conscientious Sierra Club leader. Also, I do not know whether she feels a growing and ultimately unbearable frustration at watching me hit nearly every possible snag in the river and hold up the group while becoming unsnagged. I only know that Carol and Danny finally drop behind the others and paddle over to me.

"Are you ready for rescue?" Danny calls.

"I'll take the solo boat for a while," Carol says. "It'll give you a chance to rest a bit."

"Gee. Thanks."

"We're going to take a break in a minute. Then we'll make a switch."

I have never met Danny before this trip; I have only sat in club meetings and heard him make his sales pitch for Sierra Club calendars, T-shirts, patches and other merchandise. I can vouch for his salesmanship. During the break I learn to appreciate, too, his friendliness and his generosity with paddling advice. Back on the river, I have reason to be grateful not only for his extra pair of hands and his skill in keeping the canoe on course but also for his sterling instruction in reading the river and maneuvering the boat.

"Look downstream," he instructs. "You see a lot of rocks, and a few places where there's a wide enough channel to get between them. Now where's the longest 'tongue' of dark water you can see?"

"What?"

"The longest triangle-shaped patch of dark water with its broad base upstream?"

"Over there to the left."

"Okay. Now draw."

"What's that?"

"Reach your paddle out as far to the left as you can without leaning out of the boat, and pull the water forcibly toward the boat. Right! There you go! Good! Once more, with a little more force. Good! Whee! We made it through, and we didn't even nick the rock on either side. Well done! Do you see how it goes?"

"Yeah!"

"Now Lesson Number Two. The bow paddler is responsible for seeing the underwater rocks immediately downstream from the boat and for taking the first evasive action. Your body, you see, makes a better door than window, and Cap'n Danny can't see through it. So if you see something we'd rather not run into, make a draw or a pry or a cross-draw, and when I see what you're doing, I'll follow through."

It's not long before I see we'd better go left of the rocks ahead. I reach out and draw, moving the boat to the left. Danny, with my body now not blocking his view forward, makes a corrective stroke or two, and we glide through the small drop.

"Hey, great!" he shouts. "Good maneuver!"

After Danny's friendly instruction, the remainder of the trip is infinitely more pleasant and enjoyable — for me, but not for Carol, who is both deprived of Danny's friendly and congenial company and obliged to produce double paddle-power.

The remainder of the trip is marred by an accident, not on the river but at the overnight bivouac, a broad grassy field where Carol has asked the owner's permission to camp.

Danny, walking barefoot after hanging up his shoes to dry, steps on some broken glass and cuts his foot.

Bad things happen to good people.

At the end of the trip, I have a slight altercation with Leader Carol. Meaning to be helpful, I point out to her, while all of us are crammed into someone's van, that in order to work the shuttle, it is necessary only to carry the *drivers* when retrieving the vehicles for the drive home. Green as I am, I have experienced shuttles and have some notion of their mechanics.

"Why didn't you say something before we loaded up?"

"I assumed you knew what you were doing."

Not a safe assumption, you see.

All too soon (after I became one), I learned that outings leaders are only human. ❖

—TWO - AFLOAT—
NEW ON THE GREEN

—TWO - AFLOAT—
NEW ON THE GREEN

ADVENTURE SITE
*The Green River, Polk County
North Carolina*

The New River was not the only river to which the Sierra Club introduced me. My second river trip, after I had advanced one trip above the status of utterly-green beginner, was on the Green River, in Polk County, southeast of Asheville, near the South Carolina border. I was too dependent on trip leaders in the 1970s, and thus too little aware of geographical details and too innocent of the importance of map study, to be able to tell you which section of the river we paddled or how we got there. I do recall driving through a pleasant rural area and putting in at a much-used campground on river right. <u>Now</u> I <u>know</u> that a river runner — and particularly a river trip leader — needs to know as much about roads as rivers, especially back country roads.

I can't remember who led the trip, but I have vivid memories of my paddling partner Rhonda, with whom I had shared other outdoor adventures. After one river trip, I saw myself as an experienced paddler, but it was soon clear that she considered herself (justifiably) the superior *voyageur*. Neither of us had had anything resembling formal instruction; she was relying on her memories of girl scout days; I, of course, had been neither a girl scout nor an aquatic boy scout.

✧

As soon as we put the boat in the water, it is clear we have a long way to go before becoming a team. I am in the stern and thus, by default, the prime navigator; but I am almost totally innocent of navigational strokes, even being, believe it or not, unfamiliar with the technique of ruddering. So far as I know at this stage of river awareness, the way to make the boat go straight is to have the bow and stern paddlers stroke with precisely equal power — on opposite sides of the boat. But when I try to put the principle into practice, it doesn't work a hootsworth. When the group sets off downstream, Rhonda and I are still practicing. We take our place at the end of the line of boats, trying to keep up while still learning to accommodate to one another's meager (and often contradictory) knowledge of canoe navigation.

It is a lovely summer day. I have been briefed about clothing and am prepared to "layer," my bottom layer being a pair of boxer-style nylon swimming trunks worn under a pair of light slacks of some synthetic and non-water-retentive material.

Thanks to Rhonda and other Sierra Club trippers, I have been acquiring some basic principles. Among other things, I have learned that an upset can come suddenly, without warning; therefore one makes everything as waterproof as feasible and ties everything securely into the boat. River current is sometimes swift, particularly on the Green, and will quickly carry off anything not secured: bailer, sponge, lunch, extra clothing. I have stored my quick-energy G.O.R.P. in an oatmeal box which I hope will float and which therefore I have left unsecured at my feet for quick access at moments of extreme energy depletion. Extra sweaters and shirts, I have found, are best tied where most accessible: around thwarts.

I have, I feel sure, taken care of the essentials. But it is a beautiful, warm day; the river is flowing along in a leisurely manner, and I am feeling joyous and confident. My partner and I are even beginning to accommodate to one another's canoeing skills, or lack thereof.

About mid-afternoon, when the heat of the day is becoming extreme, my partner has stripped to a skimpy two-piece bikini, and I decide to divest shirt and slacks. Alerting my partner that she is in temporary charge of navigation, I lay my paddle in the bilge (a dipping branch can flip a paddle loose if it's carelessly laid across the gunwales); I take off my shirt and tie it to the thwart and have just taken off my slacks but not yet secured them when my partner calls out: "Rapid !"

I tuck my slacks under me on the seat, pick up the paddle and kneel, preparing to run the rapid. It is such a rapid as I have never contemplated before and of which no one has warned me: a three-foot drop (though admittedly a straightforward, uncomplicated one), with a hydraulic at the base. What do I know about how to run a waterfall?

We do a very awkward flip.

I have not yet learned anything about rescues. My partner gives direction. We grab the painter and begin to pull the boat, now full of water, toward the right bank. We are wading upstream in knee-deep water, slipping and sliding over grassy-slick stream pebbles. Our aim is to arrive in shallower water or, preferably, beach on the nearby sand bar and empty the boat. Each of us has a hold on the painter. Rhonda, under five feet tall and quite tiny in other dimensions, is remarkably tough, and after heaving with double might and main, we manage to pull the boat up on the sand and gravel bar. With almost our bottom ounce of weary might and main, we raise one gunwale of the boat and empty the water.

Then we take inventory. The G.O.R.P. is missing. More importantly, the paddles are missing (except the spare, which is still tied in). Worst of all, my slacks are going down the river without me, and I have neglected to teach them to swim. As they sink and slide, they carry to the bottom my wallet and keys.

Fellow travelers retrieve the paddles. I find the G.O.R.P. in an eddy below the drop, semi-floating, semi-submerged, slowly taking on water.

❖

I never did find the slacks. Missing with the slacks: my wallet and keys.
Getting back home without car keys was a major hassle.
Replacing the contents of my wallet was major hassle.
I have not since carried either wallet or keys on the river, and I paddle in perpetual expectation of a spill, everything water-tight, shipshape and secure. ❖

—THREE - AFLOAT—
LUMBEE RIVER SERENDIPITY

—THREE - AFLOAT—
LUMBEE RIVER SERENDIPITY

ADVENTURE SITE
The Lumbee River, Scotland/ Hoke County, North Carolina

One late fall, Dick and Jane Holloman led a Sierra Club canoe trip on the Lumbee River.

Some persons say "Lumber," but I don't, since I choose to believe the name is a corruption of the name of a native American tribe centered in Robeson County, North Carolina.

The Lumbee is a beautiful "blackwater" river, stained by the tannin-rich leaves and roots of the cypress trees along its banks and in the adjoining backwaters. Some enterprising, public-spirited citizens, recognizing the value of the river as a natural, scenic and recreational resource, have created a canoe trail and then gone on to initiate both a state park and national Wild and Scenic status.

❖

By the time of the Hollomans' trip, I have begun to feel that I know all about canoeing and can handle blackwater very well. Of course, I have never seen blackwater, but somehow it doesn't sound as threatening as whitewater. After all, if there are no rapids, getting down the river without mishap should be easy as pie; right?

Wrong.

Black water and swamp do not necessarily imply slack water and smooth, easy-to-manage flat surfaces. In fact, the Lumbee is often narrow, swift and tortuous, with plenty of quick twists and turns and worse, an abundance of strainers.

No one has said much to me about strainers. These are down trees fallen across the river, blocking the path. They are shrubs and branches reaching out from shore to knock your hat off or, worse, knock your head off or toss you out of the boat. They are rock formations so tight that they do not permit a boat to pass unscathed. In short, to put the matter abstractly, a strainer allows water, being protean in nature, to flow through or around, under or over; while a boat, or more importantly, a boater, being more solidly constituted, cannot pass without serious risk of dissolution or dismemberment.

The expectation of sharp turns and the need to avoid strainers is the reason, no doubt, that Dick quizzes us as we prepare to put in. "We," in addition to Dick's wife Jane, consists of me, my son Reed, age 15, and Reed's pal Dan.

"Do you know the draw stroke?"

"Draw stroke? What's that?"

(You may remember that Danny taught me the draw stroke in **Trip One - Afloat.** But much water has gone downstream since that trip, with on my part, no refresher course and less than perfect recall).

So Dick patiently expounds to me and Reed and Dan'l the technique and the importance of the draw stroke.

How well we learn from his brief lesson will be told later.

Then Jane and Dick head down the river in their tandem canoe, hardly ever looking back to see how well we are doing. All things considered, I suppose we do all right. I am in the stern, Reed in the bow, Dan in the bilge mid boat. Reed and I wield paddles. There is a paddle for Dan'l as well, but by and large he doesn't wield it, for his doing so would be difficult to manage without a clash of paddles in mid-stroke with either Reed's or mine, or both. We decide to save Dan's paddle-power for an emergency — not that he has any great skill. This is his first river experience.

Untroubled and uncomforted by the presence of our leaders, who quickly and permanently outdistance us, we three jolly mariners content ourselves with enjoying the late fall day, warm enough in this latitude, almost in South Carolina. We paddle sometimes in the shadows of tall conifers, occasionally mixed with deciduous trees; sometimes between low banks flanked by meadows (rarely cultivated fields in this low-lying area); and sometimes in classic swamp country, where it is not always easy to distinguish main river channel and "scenic byways."

One of the revelations we are certainly not expecting is that here in swamp country we can see close up an herb usually glimpsed at great height atop giant oaks: the legendary Christmas green, mistletoe. There are places where, if we had the skill to control the boat, we could nudge the bank and reach out to pluck the festive parasite.

There comes a moment when our attention is required to cope with a less pleasant and more urgent reality. Suddenly we come face to face with a tree fallen across virtually the entire width of the river, the trunk a foot or so off the water supported by still-green branches which seem to reach out in all directions. Most importantly from our perspective, the branches reach upstream, seemingly determined to prevent any boat from coming close to the trunk without first being upset. The branches also seem to wish to scratch boaters' faces and gouge out their eyes with small and large twigs.

In a trice our boat is broadside to the current, and our faces are dodging branches. Likewise the boat is being pulled against branches and seems urgently inclined to continue downstream while we, should we continue downstream, will be at serious risk of being shredded by tree limbs. The upstream gunwale begins to dip hazardously close to the current. Should the boat begin to take on water, an upset is inevitable. We have no idea how deep the water is; we have not tested and do not wish to test either its depth or its temperature.

"Lean downstream!" I command.

It is not a moment for calm reflection. It is a moment for decisive action. Yet that decisive action must be a concerted one, all crew members acting as one. The #1 problem: to keep the boat level in spite of the current's clear desire to sweep it downstream and the limbs' wish to dip the upstream gunwale into the drink. Our hands are now employed in fending off branches; but holding branches threatens to upset the boat's center of gravity and dip the upstream gunwale underwater.

[I still, to this day, do not understand why this did not happen.]

"Keep leaning downstream!" I shout.

Clearly, as Captain and Navigator, not to mention Parent and Dan'l's Temporary Guardian *in loco parentis,* I have some responsibility to come up with a plan. Doing that in this hairy emergency is not easy. Water is flowing; the boat is tipping, and none of us has ever faced this situation before.

"Okay, guys. We have got to pull together. Keep leaning downstream, or the boat will fill. Dan, grab the spare paddle in one hand while still fending off the branches and leaning. Now, we have to do two things simultaneously, and fast. To river right, straight in front of the boat, the tree branches aren't blocking the channel, and if we make a couple of mighty strokes, we can get past the tree and into calm water. Paddles ready?"

I allow a mere moment for all of us to take a deep breath.

"Heave!" And with a mighty concerted thrust, we clear the tree and float toward the right bank, where I am able to turn the boat back parallel to the current and point it downstream.

When we have calmed our anxiety and floated again serenely down the tea-stained river, we look down and — wonder of wonders! — among the debris of twigs large and small in the bottom of the boat are several nice sprigs of mistletoe.

Reed claims that after I went back to my domicile in Charlotte and he to his in Chapel Hill, he and Dan took the mistletoe to the shopping center and made five dollars selling it to Christmas shoppers.

⬥

This, dear Reader, was the beginning of something.
To find out what, see **Trips Four - Afloat** *and* **Thirteen - Afloat.** ❖

— FOUR - AFLOAT —
Sprig Outing in Little River Swamp

— FOUR - AFLOAT —

Sprig Outing in Little River Swamp

ADVENTURE SITE
*The Upper Little River, Harnett County
North Carolina*

If you wish, you may tie this yarn to the previous one and continue knitting. If you do, you may skip a stitch; or, to switch metaphors, you may have to vault over a few years.

Reed is no longer officially a minor, and I am no longer living in Charlotte but have moved to Durham, North Carolina, where I am still active in the Sierra Club. In fact, I am instigator and chairman of a new regional group, the Headwaters Group, and am looking around for a fund-raising activity to begin the process of making the nascent organization solvent.

I have been reminded by Reed, over the years, of our "brush" with the oak-tree strainer on the Lumbee River and of his and Dan's serendipitous windfall fortune of five dollars in mistletoe sales.

❖

"Which swamp river is closest to Durham?" I ask Howard DuBose, proprietor of the River Runners' Emporium and guru to the Triangle (and the North Carolina) paddling community.

"Upper and Lower Little Rivers, tributaries of the Cape Fear, between Lillington and Fort Bragg."

That information doesn't mean much to me until Howard has supplied me with some of his free river maps and I have consulted my North Carolina county road atlas.

Then I begin canvassing my muscle-boating pals to drum up participants.

Five of us assemble on the river bank on a chill morning, the second Saturday in December.

Doubtless you have already figured out that when I say "Sprig" Outing, I am not suffering from a bad cold and am not mispronouncing the name of the vernal season but am naming the quarry of our swamp expedition: *sprigs* of mistletoe (*Viscum album* in Europe, *Phoradendron flavescens* in the United States).

❖ 26 WILDERNESS ADVENTURES: AFOOT & AFLOAT   **115**

We are paddling two tandem canoes and a kayak. Kendy is the kayaker. Dave Knowles and I are paddling his red *Old Town* canoe. Gerald the icthyologist and Kendy's husband Rick, the anthropologist, will be lumbering downstream in a borrowed blunderbuss Grumman aluminum boat.

Gerald has ulterior motives. He has a grant to discover just how endangered or conversely, how endemic, is a certain species of tiny guppy-like creature. Neither he nor Rick is an accomplished canoeist, but both are game. David, a biology teacher in a local junior high school, is an accomplished canoeist and in general a skilled outdoors man.

The first part of the trip goes well. We are warm enough under a partly sunny sky, with only a slight breeze; and we garner sufficient mistletoe to feel that the trip has been a reasonable success. In fact, the trip goes so well that, after we spend time at the proposed take-out using Gerald's kick-seine to check for the presence of his little fish, we find that we still have some daylight — and, more importantly, warming sunlight — remaining before discretion and the approach of cold darkness will warn us off the river. We put our heads together and decide to continue downstream to the next convenient take-out. It is not a good decision. We have not scouted the next section.

We soon regret our intrepidity. The river, which until now has been broad and relatively tranquil, soon narrows, twists, picks up speed and is fraught with strainers — branches reaching out from the banks. The first to test the survivability in the 42° water are Gerald and Rick in the Grumman. The swiftness and the need to maneuver quickly prove to be beyond their skill, and they are dumped into the frigid water. Then the current carries Dave's boat under a tree branch, and I, unwisely, grab it to try to persuade it from decapitating me; its response is to dump both me and Dave into the river. Greenhorn that I am, I lose track of my paddle, while Dave, a more seasoned practitioner, manages to retain all the essentials that aren't tied down: his hat, his glasses and his paddle. We somehow recover sufficiently to retrieve both the paddle I've let go of and even the aluminum boat, which Gerald and Rick have abandoned in their haste to withdraw their frigid bodies from the comfortless river. It takes some furious paddling to overtake the Grumman. The Grumman's paddles, though, go down the stream of time. Then it takes some furious paddling for Dave and me to struggle back upstream to where Rick and Gerald are climbing the bank.

Meanwhile Gerald, and particularly Rick, have become aware that Kendy, witnessing the distress of each pair of tandem boaters, has decided to arrest her downstream progress. She has grabbed a branch low enough to the river to be reachable from her low-to-the-water kayak and, recalling the First Principle of Boating Rescue, has refused to let go of her paddle or to make a wet exit from the boat. Unfortunately, the result is that the combination of downstream current and her grip on the branch submerges both the boat and the boater. Rick, seeing that the current is causing Kendy's head to plunge at times under the surface, has gone to Kendy's rescue while Dave and I are hauling the heavy Grumman upstream to a decent landing place river right.

Needless to say, once we all get together on the bank, at the edge of some farmer's cornfield, we quickly make the decision to abort the trip: the Grumman obviously can't continue without paddles. Luckily, Dave has done enough map study to know quickly in which direction to hike in order to fetch his truck.

Dave, by his example, has given me a valuable lesson (HANG ON TO YOUR PADDLE !) There now ensues a scene which supplies another forever-memorable teaching about winter paddling and about gender considerations in the paddling community. Without any noticeable hesitation, Kendy pulls out her tiny dry-bag from the kayak and, laying it at her feet, proceeds to strip down to her bikini and pull on the dry clothes from her little bag. By the time she and Dave take off to hike to his truck, she is dry and warmly dressed, something the others of us envy long before Kendy and Dave disappear from view. Actually, having taken seriously the wisdom imparted by a speaker at a club meeting, an outfitter up to speed on the latest high-tech clothing, I have dressed sensibly in polypropylene and am soon dried and warmed by the now-declining sun. Gerald and Rick shiver in their cotton longies.

In fact, so comfortable am I after only a few minutes that, while waiting for Dave and Kendy to return in the truck, I climb a couple of the holly trees that are growing profusely on the bank; and soon I am tossing down nice holly boughs for my buddies to bag (I have remembered my pruner). The bags of mistletoe, having been well tied into each boat, go home with us as well. Thus we have the merchandise which our little club requires and, in addition, bright holly berries with which to "deck the halls."

✦

If memory serves, we took home and sold to a florist four tall grocery bags of mistletoe at fifteen dollars per bag, putting $60 into the treasury for conservation work.

This figure does not take into account the cost to Gerald and Rick of replacing the lost paddles. ❖

—FIVE - AFLOAT—
SEARCHING FOR THE GIANT CYPRESS

—FIVE - AFLOAT—
Searching for the Giant Cypress

ADVENTURE SITE
Merchants Millpond, Gates County
North Carolina

I've done quite a bit of thinking about the meaning of "adventure." What are its constituent elements? How can I tell whether I'm having something that can legitimately be called an ADVENTURE?

If we set out the four "D's," we are coming close to identifying adventure's essence. These four "D's" are:

DANGER,
DOUBT,
DISCOMFORT and
DISCOVERY.

Not all of those elements are present in the same proportions in every one of life's adventures.

In **Trip Twelve - Afoot** I have actually alluded to a rather hazardous situation at Merchants Millpond State Park. Most of my dozens of visits there have involved more discovery — and sheer pleasure in a unique natural environment — than either discomfort or danger. But there is something about my experiences in this small but unique park that causes me to add a fifth "D" to my definition of adventure:

DESIRE.

In **Listening to Chris,** I have described the park, but I haven't begun to describe all the many visits I have made there in various seasons of the year. I'll allude here to only a pair of the dozens of visits I've made to the pond.

The first time I visited the park, it had been newly created; had only one ranger, Cecil Frost; and was largely undeveloped. It did have the family campground, and when I camped there with the Sierra Club group from Charlotte, we were visited by Cecil at our evening campfire. Spellbound, we forgot the hardness of our log seats as he gave us an orientation, a description and a challenge.

He talked history, of the pond, the area and the entire East Coast; politics (of state parks); and the geography and ecology of the mill pond. Then he challenged us.

The Europeans, moving inland from the coast, cut all the timber within reach — for housing, for ship-building and to make space for the cultivation of food crops. The ecology of the state park was created by damming Lassiter Creek and flooding the area in order to float out the huge boles of cypress (genus *Cupressus*) and tupelo (*Nyssa aquatica*). The area of the park surrounding the pond was not logged and thus can boast one of the few remaining stands of virgin timber on the Eastern Seaboard.

And evidently the loggers overlooked — or could not reach — one huge cypress tree on the banks of Lassiter Creek, upstream from the present pond. And so it stands: a lone Virgin Giant looking down on the colossal stumps in the pond.

If we could find the place where Lassiter Creek widens to form the pond, Cecil told us, and if we could distinguish the main channel from all the false ones at the head of the pond, and if it weren't too wet or too dry a spring; and if the beavers weren't building in the main channel — we might travel by boat up the creek to find that giant cypress tree. I developed a DESIRE, which over the years became almost an obsession, to find the channel, the creek and the cypress tree. After many visits to the park I began to feel comfortable enough in the park, on the pond, in the water and in a canoe to pursue that obsession.

If you've ever been in a cypress and tupelo swamp, you have some idea of its eeriness, of the gloomy impressions conveyed by the festoons of Spanish moss, by the sameness of the thick stumps and scattered hummocks, the lack of clear landmarks or water-marks to guide one's explorations. The matter is complicated by the crescent shape of the pond: one can't pursue a course for long toward any particular point of the compass. From one visit to another, the beavers may have abandoned or relocated a lodge one has used as a guide.

All of this made it more challenging to pursue the goal that Cecil introduced in his talk early in my boating career. To find beavers one had to venture out at the optimum time of day — dawn or dusk — and leave the security of the buoy-marked main-traveled "roads" of the pond. To search upstream in Lassiter, one had to wander even farther afield and study quite subtle water currents.

✧

But the day comes when I am ready. Dressed in my river clothes, which are allowed to get wet and muddy; and traveling alone (who else could be found crazy enough to undertake such a mission) I set out from the family campground "bound for adventure." I have the DESIRE; I am ready for a great DISCOVERY or two; I have substantially overcome DOUBT by studying the area for years and don't greatly mind undergoing some DISCOMFORT and maybe even a bit of DANGER in the enterprise.

The first two or three green buoys, some of them now fading to yellow, bleached by the sun, soaked in rain and pond water and occasionally covered with algae or mere green slime, are in place merely to lead the innocent boater to the center of the pond. Where the next couple of floats, looking for all the world like leftover gallon milk jugs, begin turning to the right, toward the boat landing and park headquarters, I must turn left, "upstream" on the seemingly streamless, undifferentiated, tranquil pond — where innocent water lilies (*Nymphaea odorata*) harbor placid fishes and where low stumps and floating logs accommodate sedentary sun-bathing tortoises. Leaving the comfort of the buoys, I start in earnest to pursue my GREAT ADVENTURE.

Paddling on my strong side, the right, I grit my teeth, make a couple of sweep strokes and bid the buoys Good-bye. I am headed away from the park office, "upstream," still not convinced that a stream feeds this placid pond. I notice the water-lilies, which are more numerous here than in the "lower" pond. Then I see a great pile of sticks and branches rising three or four feet above the surface, and it takes me several seconds to think "Oh ! Beaver lodge !" and begin being excited at the DISCOVERY.

A moment later, I discover another lodge; and then a third. One key to continuing "upstream" is to avoid turning toward either the right "shore" or the left "shore," where one can become bogged down among cypress trees in the bankside shallows. But to distinguish these right and left "shores" is tricky.

I try to pay attention to currents. This can be done by feeling the effect of the water on the sides of the boat — if the dying of the breeze permits this subtle influence to be detectable. One can also, in the absence of that same complicating breeze, observe the underwater drift of the watery grasses; of the algae-specks on the surface; or the floating stems of water-lilies.

I have no compass. It might or might not help. I have, or thought I had, in my head, a general map of the pond. It, too, is probably useless. Dead reckoning and close observation are primary. And, by golly, the pond does seem to be narrowing. The distance between the right and left tree lines seems to be diminishing, and the water lily territory is giving way to something which begins to have the feel of an "upstream" tree bank. The problem now is that there isn't only one — there are several — candidates for "the" way to somehow penetrate that upstream bank.

I experiment with first one and then another potential channel, constantly trying to observe evidences of greater or lesser flow.

I encounter another beaver lodge blocking a "channel" which, probably fox-and-sour-grapes-like, I decide can't be the right one. Back-tracking, I head between tightly spaced trees to cross what feels like a cross-channel entrance to another channel. It, too, has a noticeable current and seems to be a promising candidate. Soon I come to what appears to be an incipient beaver-dam: a few boughs lying loosely on the surface. Gathering speed, I try to make a run through — and get stuck. After back-paddling, I try again, this time making what I hope is a powerful run — and get across the branches, though the last stroke before the boat floats free feels as if it were pushing the boat through thick pudding! The searching, I begin to feel, is at least as much fun as the finding could ever be.

Soon I come to a place where the current is a mere trickle, too shallow to float even my canoe's three-inch draft.

This is not the day, apparently; this is not the spring, when I am destined to find the Giant Cypress. Maybe some other time.

❖

I haven't yet found that Giant Cypress.

I'm glad it's out there — if it still is.

Knowing about it, I'll always have a reason to go back, and something to live for: the four (or is it five?) "D's" of Adventure: DANGER, DOUBT, DISCOMFORT, DISCOVERY — and yes! surely DESIRE. ❖

— SIX - AFLOAT —
OKEFENOKEE I:
HIGH POINT ON BIG WATER LAKE

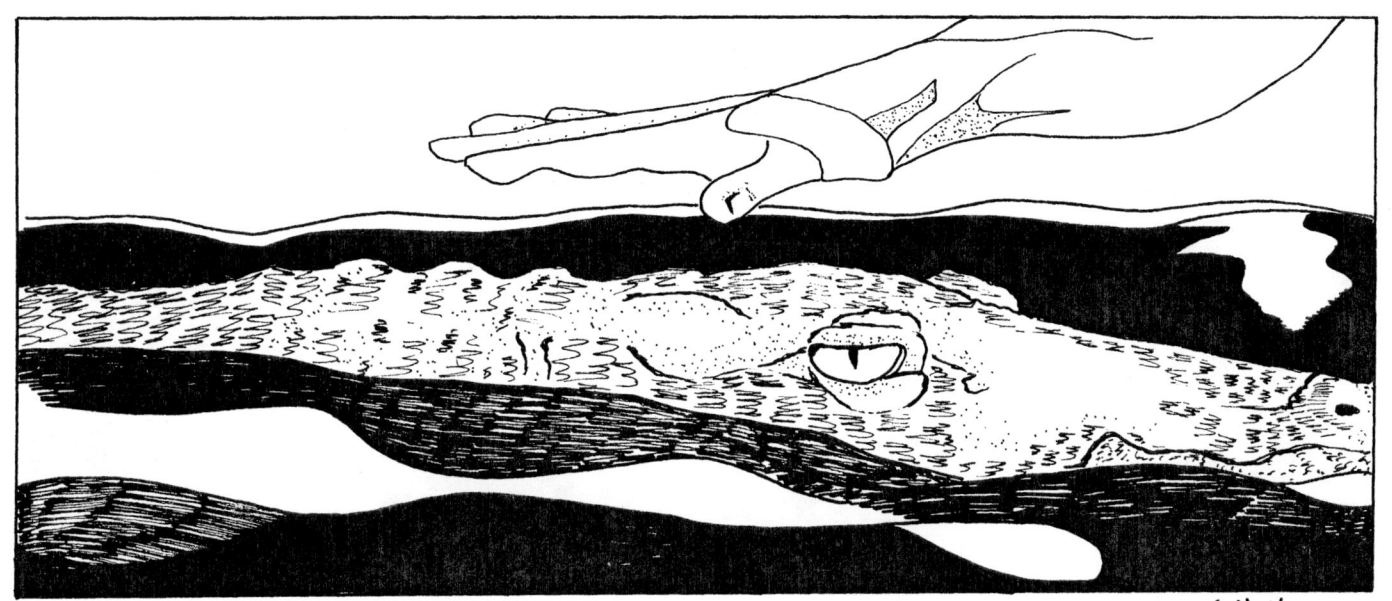

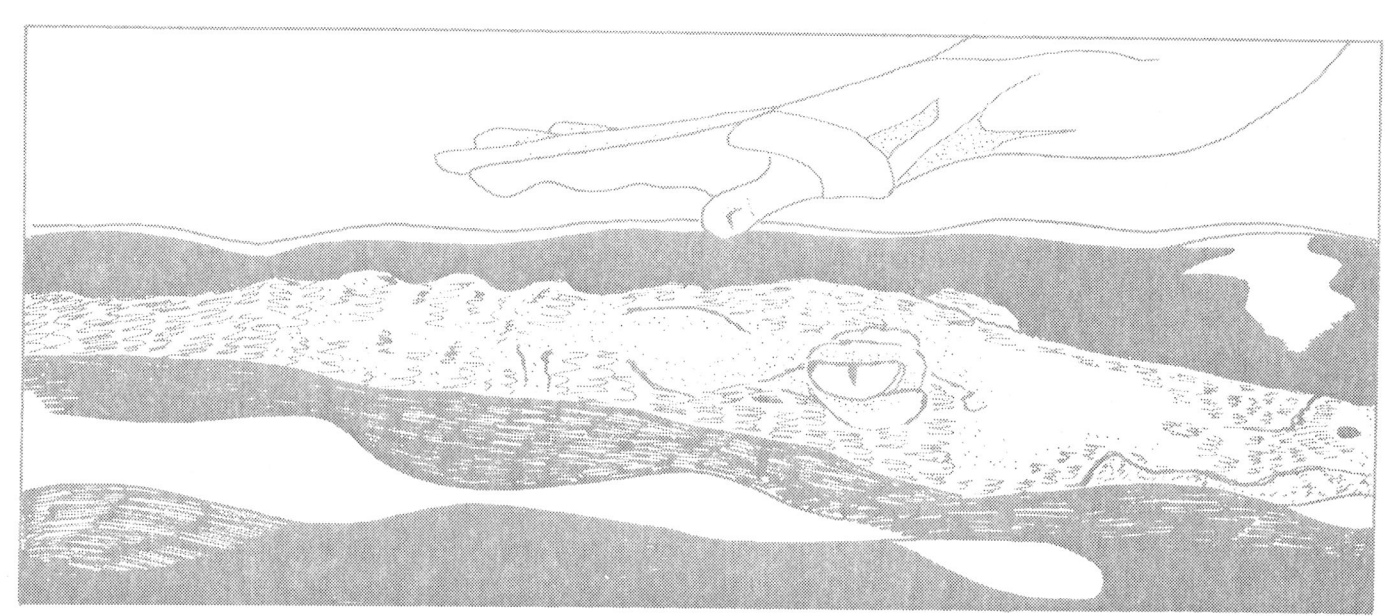

—SIX - AFLOAT—
OKEFENOKEE I:
HIGH POINT ON BIG WATER LAKE

ADVENTURE SITE
Okefenokee National Wildlife Refuge
Florida/Georgia

A generation ago everyone "knew" about the Okefenokee Swamp: it was the home of Pogo the Possum, the comic-strip created by Walt Kelly. I didn't meet Pogo there, but I did make the acquaintance of many other wild creatures.

Cartoons aside, the Okefenokee National Wildlife Refuge is a real place, one of the few natural areas left in the United States, the largest and best preserved swamp in the country and one of the most primitive on the planet. When the Atlantic Ocean extended 75 miles west beyond its present boundary, the Okefenokee was part of the ocean floor. It is now a saucer-like depression a mere 103 to 123 feet above sea level, overlain by a peat bog. The peat is thin in some places and as thick as 20 feet in others. When peat surfaces, it floats, supporting a varying growth of vegetation but remaining unstable. Having stepped on the "quivering earth" (the meaning of <u>Okefenokee</u> in the Choctaw language), I can testify that it is not always able to support the weight of a person.

Higher than most of the surrounding territory, the Okefenokee depends on local rainfall for its replenishment. In the swamp are formed two rivers: the eastward-flowing St. Marys, which forms the Georgia-Florida border and empties into the Atlantic Ocean, and the Suwannee, which, draining more of the Refuge, flows westerly and southerly into the Gulf of Mexico.

Of the 438,000 acres in the Okefenokee Swamp, the 60 lakes comprise only about 1000 acres of open water. Most of the remaining area is "prairie," shallow water with lush growth of aquatic plants dotted with "hammocks," on which shrubs and even small trees have established themselves. There is an occasional island, sometimes supporting huge moss-draped cypress trees.

❖

About 396,000 acres in the interior of the swamp are included in the Wildlife Refuge. Actually, it was largely in order to protect the creatures in places like the Okefenokee that the Endangered Species Act was passed. Here in the swamp are found 225 species of birds, 32 of amphibians, 58 of reptiles, 34 of fishes. The alligators, once close to extinction, have now been restored to number more than 10,000. I may have seen well over 5 percent of them on my first trip into the swamp with my son, a Sierra Club friend and her daughter over the long Easter week-end of 1979.

❖

The leader of this trip meets us at the trailhead, Kingfisher Landing, with some bad news and some good news. The bad news is that his wife, who is with him, has recently undergone a miscarriage and is in no condition to paddle for three days in the Okefenokee. The good news is that he has brought his two canoes, will launch us in them and will meet us at Stephen Foster State Park, on the western edge of the swamp, where he and his wife will be camping while we four stalwarts paddle the 31 miles of canoe trail, camping two nights on the way.

Part of the first day has been consumed by travel to the put-in. We have started from Charlotte the night before, traveled all night (driving in shifts) and launched not long before noon on Saturday. With John's blessing (and his boats and other gear), we paddle away from Kingfisher Landing on the well-marked Red Trail, one of six such trails in the Refuge totaling 100 miles. Signs a mile apart inform us how far we have paddled. Our destination for Day One is Maul Hammock, where a platform built several feet above the water is to be our camping place.

Topographic maps, with their variety of symbols for different kinds of landscape and waterscape, can only begin to suggest the variety of scenes through which we pass. At Kingfisher Landing (called "Kings Landing" on the U.S.G.S. map) the cleared land ends. The ten-foot-wide waterway on which we launch runs straight southwesterly for .4 mile with what the map calls "wood cover" on both banks, paralleling an old tramway (logging was carried out here before the area was closed to development). Then, for a mile, the narrowed boat trail sweeps in a broad arc northwesterly, with mostly "woods cover" on the right and, on the left, the edges of and openings into the open water of Trout Lake, Double Lakes, Christmas Lake, and Ohio Lake, where we pass "aquatic plants interspersed with reeds and tree growths" and "grasses and scattered brush." These descriptions, quoted from the U.S.G.S. quad, give but a scant impression of the thickness of the forest cover; the vastness of the open prairies; the variety of the pond scenes; the myriad land and water plants; the beauty of trailside wild flowers and the excitement of flushing alligator after alligator sunning on the banks.

Reed, at 17, is a strong paddler, supplying power in the bow while I act as stern navigator. In the two-boat flotilla, ours leads. In the other canoe Rhonda, the mother, my Green River partner in **Trip Two - Afloat**, occupies the stern. Daughter Cindy, a young woman of perhaps 19, considerably less experienced with a paddle than her mother, does her best to cope in the bow. Both of these women are petite and, coming up short in muscle-power, constantly have difficulty keeping up. Reed and I, leading, usually have first opportunity to view the azure-colored orchid, the odd fungus, the passing gar-fish or the 'gator sunning on the bank. Rhonda and Cindy, on the other hand, get to enjoy an experience which Reed and I miss: the snake dropping into their boat.

"What do we do now?" Cindy wants to know, her voice quivering slightly. She has some reason to be nervous; the snake has dropped between her and her mother; she can't see it as she faces forward; therefore she doesn't know which way the creature may be headed or whether it's one of the poisonous ones.

I try to be comforting.

"Let it alone until it decides to walk the plank."

Instead Rhonda, using her paddle as a prod, guides the snake overboard. I never get close enough to see it. The only snakes I am able to see on the trip are those in the ranger's slide show at Stephen Foster Park at the end of the trip.

We are enjoying the unique natural beauty of the watery world through which we travel, but we meet one brief annoyance and are troubled with a nagging concern.

We are traveling on the Red Trail, which crosses the swamp from east to west. Use permits are issued to only one party each day in each direction on each section of trail. Thus we meet only one other canoe party each day of our three-day trip, making for a fine feeling of being "away from it all," on our own in the wilderness.

But there's a catch.

Only in the very interior of the Refuge are motorboats excluded. Thus on the first and third days of our trip we also meet a party of motorboaters. We aren't prepared for that.

Innocently paddling, we begin to hear the sound of motors, and before long three — count 'em — 3 — motorboats come zooming along at an unconscionably high rate of speed, nearly ramming our boat, startling Reed, setting up a wake that threatens to swamp both our boats and evoking a stream of invective from me.

In a moment the annoyance has vanished. The wake subsides, and even the sound is receding rapidly. The wilderness is again pristine, and we are its first visitors.

The other negative has been a constant from the time of launch: the pressure of time. We made a late start and have ten miles to go before dark. Remember, now, that these are flat water miles, not river miles with a current to assist. No drifting or coasting is involved in paddling the flat water of the Red Trail. And we are under pressure from another source: rain is threatening, and we want to arrive at Maul Hammock Lake before the deluge. I call back to the ladies, who are lagging some yards behind and are clearly laboring.

"How would it be if we attached a line from our boat to yours?"

"What do you think we are — weaklings?" Rhonda is laughing, but it is clear that I have offended her feminine dignity.

"Male chauvinist pig!" says Cindy. She is half-smiling and yet fully serious.

The women paddle harder. Clearly, though, they are tiring.

Why would we not consider dividing up the muscle-power, placing a male person and a female person in each boat?

Because Reed has never paddled with nor even ever met Rhonda or Cindy before this trip. Because the younger two paddlers are still, so to speak, undergoing orientation by Dad and Mom respectively and are not yet ready to experiment with switching partners.

It isn't long, though, before fatigue and the thickening of the black clouds drive us to tie a knot between our stern painter and the other boat's bow line.

When we arrive at Maul Hammock at six o'clock, the wind is picking up and rain is imminent.

We meet new marvels.

The canoe trail user in the Refuge is required to carry a portable toilet — and to use it while afloat. At most camping platforms a one-holer is available. The little privy at Maul Hammock, we find, is a fancy chemical toilet in a sturdy metal building resembling a telephone booth. It comes in handy later as a raccoon-resistant food safe. By morning each of us has had a midnight encounter with one or more of these clever, thieving rascals.

It rains early, but not before we have finished supper, washed the dishes, put away the food and stowed the dish-washing water to carry home. No dumping is permitted in the swamp; this is to remain a natural area. In a gathering darkness that is punctuated by wind-gusts, we hold a brief session of shared outdoor adventure stories. One gust carries a hint of rain across our roofed but open-sided camping platform. And then another. And another. Finally, the yawns which each of us has been suppressing swell and triumph, too powerful to be hidden discreetly behind a fist to the face. We retire to the tents and bed down. All night long our Mother Nature plays one of my favorite melodies: a tune titled

"Rain on the Roof." I love that song — when I'm snug and dry.

The black clouds are gone by morning; the day dawns pink and lovely in a sky clear and blue.

The second day's trip spans the distance from Maul Hammock to Big Water Lake, crossing or passing Bird Lake, Sapling Prairie and Dinner Pond, over open water and through areas thick with water lilies. We meander through many narrow channels among trees. The climax of Day Two is Big Water Lake, through which we need to pass just before our arrival at the night's shelter.

Day One, with its shared experiences of dealing with wildlife, time-pressure and threatening weather, has begun the bonding process. Evening One, with its shared adventure stories, has advanced the process. Morning Two, more leisurely under a bright sun and puffy clouds, warms the blood and the hearts; opens pores, sweat glands and personalities. During our Day Two lunch stop, I suggest we switch partners. I paddle with Rhonda, Reed with Cindy. Toward the end of the day, all of us experience something literally unique. At least, I for one have never experienced anything like it before or since.

Big Water Lake would be classified by the topographic map as open water, but as we experience it, it is not exactly that. For one thing, its surface, except for a small open patch in the center, is covered with floating water lilies (*Nymphaea mexicana*). In the brilliant sunshine, their bright yellow blossoms are lovely to behold; <u>and</u> their surface-occupying broad leaves and paddle-snarling long stems are a serious deterrent to navigation. And the lilies are not the only navigational hazard at Big Water Lake. The site has evidently, just before our arrival, been reserved for a conventicle of politic alligators! I have never again seen such a congregation, though I have been back to that site since, at about the same time of year. Until now we have seen only the odd old bull basking in the sun on the bank or on a log; here the alligators' floating hulks, in a variety of sizes, are so thick upon the surface and among the lilies, that we have difficulty finding a place to dip the paddle. Reed and Cindy are separated from Rhonda and me by several hundred yards, and, like any parent, I suppose, I worry more about their safety in this situation than I do about my own. Will they exercise good judgment in threading their way through the maze of bony spines and leathery tails? The thrill I am experiencing is tempered by apprehension for my own, my friends' and especially my son's safety.

Unbelievably, the thrilling afternoon with its fair lilies and its frightening reptiles is followed by an equally memorable evening and night. Alligators, I learn, provide a fine barking bass continuo to the tenor and contralto, the soprano and the sopranino of frogs, fowl, crickets and sundry other nameless singers, who keep up an all-night symphony *fortissimo sostenuto* every bit as enjoyable as the previous night's "Rain on the Roof" lullaby — and as powerful in its way as Beethoven's Choral Symphony.

On Day Three I take my turn at paddling with Cindy. We begin with me in the stern threading a tortuous gloom of moss-draped cypresses. When we reach the broad Suwannee, I yield the stern to Cindy as we float down to Stephen Foster Park. The Middle Fork of the Suwannee is formed by many tiny rivulets flowing from the area of Dinner Pond and culminating at Big Water Lake. After a brief passage through classic cypress swamp, our Middle Fork suddenly debouches into a busy, broad Suwannee, where we are challenged to cope with traffic. Other boats, including power boats with perilous wakes, ply these broad waters in both directions. It is important that we hue carefully to a safe course.

My brain is fully challenged because I have insisted on letting Cindy try a new experience: paddling in the stern, with me in the bow trying to navigate by telling her which kinds of strokes to use. With eyes forward to chart our course, I cannot *see* what she is doing; I must judge by the movement of the boat and the situation ahead which direction to give.

"J-stroke, Cindy! Another one! Another. Steady as she goes. I mean power-stroke. All right! Now, how about a sweep stroke? Another one. Stronger. Now, paddle forward."

After a mile of this kind of navigation, we make a left turn into the long canal that leads to the boat landing at Foster Park. Leader John and wife are waiting for us.

❖

I don't claim to have been the perfectly communicative parent to my son, but I have followed one practice that has produced some interesting results over the years. I have made a practice of encouraging him to think about his experiences and their meaning.

"What was the high point of the trip for you, Reed?" I ask him on our way home in the car.

My son has often surprised me, but no answer has surprised — or simultaneously distressed and delighted — more than his answer to this one.

He says, "Do you remember when I was paddling with Cindy at Big Water Lake?"

"Yes?"

"Well, once, when the alligators were thick around the boat, I reached out of the canoe and put my hand on the head of an alligator."

❖

So far as I know, he's never been able to top that one; and neither have I. ❖

— SEVEN - AFLOAT —
Facing Wind and Tide

—SEVEN - AFLOAT—
FACING WIND AND TIDE

ADVENTURE SITE
*Hammocks Beach State Park
North Carolina*

Against the advice of my editor, I here include some pages of pre-trip minutiae. Any reader anxious to get afloat on the Intracoastal Waterway may skip immediately to page 139, the paragraph beginning "The plan for Saturday is to paddle to the [Bear] Island."

— F.A.

Why would I wish to bore you with the details of trip planning when you are eager to get on out there into the wilderness? I'll try to justify my decision.

I have dedicated this book to the selfless mentors who provided me with my outdoor initiation and to those who may choose to do the same for others in the future. The next couple of pages should give you some idea of the personal sacrifices and headaches involved when they lead such trips. I do not know the details of what others have done to prepare for wilderness forays; the best I can do is tell you what I know: how I have prepared.

Ordinarily I've led trips to places where some Sierra Club or Canoe Club leader has taken me, places I've enjoyed and wish to share as others have shared with me. In addition, for many years I have kept a file of places where I'd like to go, just in case the opportunity might present. When I've accumulated enough information, I've started to think seriously about actually leading a trip there, whether or not I've actually been there myself.

Keeping files was never the pleasantest aspect of trip leadership, but I have accepted it because it seemed a necessary part of the task.

Scouting, another prelude to leading others into the wilderness, can be fun, especially when undertaken with an adventurous, resourceful and skilled companion. I have had several wonderfully hardy and eager scouting partners. But even scouting is often preceded by hours of fact-finding by letter and telephone, and by buying and studying maps.

Scouting is often followed by the writing of trip descriptions for publication in newspapers and newsletters; by taking calls and recording phone numbers of would-be participants; by patient explanations and discreet inquiries to discover whether the caller has the requisite motivation and skills; and by exasperated listening as late callers say they can't make the trip after all; or by waiting at the trailhead for fellow travelers to show up late — or not at all — though they swore they'd be there.

The trip to Bear Island, in Hammocks Beach State Park, is one I led without first scouting it. That is not to say I was unprepared. My recall of the process of preparing is aided by the twenty pieces of paper in my file marked "Hammocks Beach July 22-24, 1988" and by six photographs in my album for that period.

Here is a list of the items in my file:

1. Hand-written letter from park ranger at Hammocks Beach State Park dated February 24, 1988, enclosing:
2. Hammocks Beach State Park Ferry Schedule
3. Camping Information, Hammocks Beach State Park, Bear Island
4. Brochure and map of Bear Island
5. A more detailed brochure and map
6. Slip of paper with Superintendent's and Ranger's names and telephone numbers
7. Draft of trip notice for newsletter of Headwaters Group of the Sierra Club
8-9. Two-sheet draft of trip information for participants
10. Slip of paper: "Sue/Hammocks 362-5363"
11. Slip of paper: noting phone call to Jesse Hines, Sr., park ranger
12. Slip of paper noting phone call from John R—, prospective trip participant
13. Slip of paper noting phone call from Sylvia S—, prospective trip participant
14. Note from Jeff C—, prospective trip participant
15. Another hand-written note from Jesse Hines
16-20. Original, carbon and two photocopies of informational letter and map for trip participants
21. Greatly scratched-out and corrected trip roster headed "July 22-24, Hammocks," containing 16 names (ultimately 6 persons made the trip).

Do you begin to see some of the headaches involved in trip leadership and some of the reasons it's not easy to find outings leaders (never mind finding <u>good</u> leaders)?

The letter from Jesse Hines says:

Thank you for your interest in Hammocks Beach State Park as a potential site for your club. A canoe outing would be quite feasible; however, canoes can't be carried on the ferry. Your group may either follow the ferry or someone will direct you. The canoes may be put over at the boat ramp at the park. There will also be someone to take your group on a nature hike.

Due to the dates given, you will have to contact the office as soon as possible in order to reserve a campsite. Enclosed is information on camping and ferry schedule. If you have any further questions, please contact the office.

The brochure opens by quoting John Burroughs (1886): "The Voice of the Sea is Unlike Any Other Sound in Nature." It continues by describing the island:

A wide expanse of sand stretching almost four miles along the Atlantic coast provides the tranquil setting for one of the most beautiful beaches on the North Carolina coast. Bear Island, lying between Bogue and Bear Inlets, forms a major part of Hammocks Beach State Park. The island is separated from the mainland by an expanse of Salt Marshes, tidal estuarine creeks and the Intracoastal Waterway. Within its 892 acres are a diversity of habitats; bare and sparsely vegetated dunes rising to heights of sixty feet, dense thickets, a remnant of maritime forest, tidal mud flats and open beach.

Under the heading "Flora and Fauna." the leaflet tells us that the island has been nominated as a National Natural Landmark for its sea oats, wax myrtle, red cedar, live oak, pennywort, deer, raccoons, an occasional bobcat, egrets, herons and nesting terns and shore birds. Then,

The beach becomes a very special place during the warm nights from May through September. Bear Island ranks as one of the most important nesting places in North Carolina for the endangered loggerhead sea turtle. Female loggerheads come ashore on summer nights to deposit their eggs in the warm sands. Visitors should not disturb these or any other wildlife in the park. Activities on the beach at night (lights, noise, etc.) should be kept to a minimum during this period. Camping is not permitted during nights of the full moon in June, July and August to ensure the continued use of this beach as a sea turtle sanctuary.

After this description, I was determined to treat myself and others to the experience of exploring Bear Island.

The following hand-written notice was published in *The Source*, newsletter of the Headwaters Group.

July 22-24 Hammocks Beach State Park Canoe / Hike / Swim / Overnight. — Enjoy the isolation of this barrier island, aided by insights of Club and/or Park naturalists. The last ferry leaves at 6:00 p. m.; then the island belongs to campers and even wilder creatures. Call or write — [etc. etc.]

Once the notice was published, the telephone began ringing. Some callers were serious; some were not. There are in this world a great many armchair nature enthusiasts; they are enamored of the <u>idea</u> of being in the wild; they love to look in the mirror and imagine they are seeing the image of an energetic outdoor adventurer. But if you hint at exertion, perspiration, danger, hardship or discomfort as the cost of adventure, you may turn them off in a hurry. You can often turn them off merely by mentioning that the trip may call for a degree of skill or minimal clothing or equipment of a certain type. But it is better to screen on the telephone than at the trailhead or *in medias res*. And of course, even after I've done my screening, the enrollees continued to screen themselves.

"*Oh, dear. That's the week-end Aunt Suzy said she might stop on her way to —*" or
"*Honey, wouldn't you rather —*" or
"*Doesn't the long-range forecast say —*" or
"*I feel a cold coming on.*"

The eighteen spaces on the trip roster form filled quickly and then, nearly as quickly, the drop-outs began calling. An informational letter went to twelve persons. It listed their names, addresses and telephone numbers, "to facilitate car pooling (and paddling match-ups)" and, for those eager to get direct information "from the horse's mouth," the address of the park ranger. It also described the PLAN:

Camp Friday at Cedar Point Campground, on the White Oak River (50 campsites, $3 fee; drinking water, toilets). On Saturday morning. drive to Park office; launch boats; follow ferry route to Bear Island (see enclosed map). Should be about two- or three-hour paddle, After landing at (or near) boat dock, we'll have to tote camping gear some distance; say, half a mile, to Group Camp Site "A," "B" or "C." Pack gear in back pack and travel light. We'll set up camp and be free to explore, swim or nap . . . . Maybe we'll be lucky enough to observe turtle hatching activity. At some point a ranger will give us interpretive words. After exploring on foot or by canoe Sunday, and a refreshing swim in the Atlantic Ocean, we'll pack, launch and depart!

After giving directions to Cedar Point and Hammocks Beach, the sheet told what to bring:

. . . canoe; tent; back pack; day pack; old clothes that don't mind getting wet and muddy, including hat; sun screen; insect repellent; food; water; bathing suit; nature guides; rain gear; flashlight . . .

When Carol Ann called me (another Carol, not the club officer and leader of **Trips Eight - Afoot** and **One - Afloat**), I was quite taken with her enthusiasm. She, in turn, was impressed when I did not hesitate to accept her proposed fellow traveler.

"Is my daughter welcome?"

"How old?"

"Eight,"

"It's a family outing."

What impressed me about Bob's call was his description of his paddling skill and experience.

I never did manage to link up with any of the other participants at Cedar Point Campground, on the White Oak River. My sole companions in the tent, in addition to the odd mosquito, were the "no-see-ums." Actually, the latter were not so bad; a fellow in the campground gave me good advice about no-see-ums (in case you aren't familiar with these creatures, they're annoying as gnats but infinitely smaller — small enough to pass through the finest mosquito net on the best state-of-the-art tent).

"Wear something white," he said. "That'll keep 'em off you."

I rarely wear anything when I sleep, especially in the summer, but since hearing that advice, I carry white sheets for summer camping. My winter bag is too warm for summer use anyway.

❖

THE PLAN FOR SATURDAY morning is to paddle to the island on the outgoing tide. The sun's rising this Saturday is obscured by clouds, and by the time of my arrival at park headquarters, it is completely overcast and looking as if it will rain any second. Cooling my heels while waiting, I check our camping reservations at the office and re-check tide charts. High tide has occurred earlier, but we can still catch a bit of ebb-tide if we start soon. Just before nine o'clock, a steady drizzle begins descending, and three boaters arrive. Carol Ann, daughter Erica and traveling companion Bob have had difficulty locating the recommended campground and have spent the night in a different one. When John and Monique arrive a few minutes later, it is raining hard.

What to do? We gather on the covered front porch of the public rest room to hold a conference. It becomes an intermittent and prolonged consultation punctuated by the process of getting acquainted. Erica, at eight years of age, shows remarkable patience.

Eventually, two realities converge: the adults' impatience and a break in the precipitation. We unload the boats from our vehicles and carry them to the dock.

I have feared that I would be paddling alone. Since Bob has traveled and camped with Carol and Erica, I suppose he'll want to be in the boat with them, too; and in fact it is clear he prefers that arrangement. Carol, however, has a different idea. She has decided during our first telephone conversation that I am "her man"; anyone who enthusiastically accepts Erica's participation in the outing is the right paddling partner for Mama. Furthermore, it is clear to me that Bob is physically the stronger of the two of us and a more experienced canoer, making it logical for him to take Erica in the bow of his boat.

The harbor at the park faces and opens on the Intracoastal Waterway. We watch two departing ferry boats turn right (south) on the Waterway. With that guidance and the map on our park brochures, we feel oriented.

I give the standard Sierra Club outings leaders' orientation speech about the importance of staying within seeing and hearing distance of one another; and we launch. I have been in a boat once before on the Intracoastal Waterway — at Kissimmee, Florida, where the narrowness of the channel and the presence of many motorboats with their many and sharp wakes and of inboard yachts with their competing wakes made for a spine-jarring experience.

Here the Waterway is wider, and the ferries, almost the sole craft on the water, other than our three canoes, out of regard for the canoes' lightness and inferior handling powers under muscle power, watch their wakes, slowing while passing us. Ferries pass going in both directions, their passengers evidently amused at our crab-like strokes and gastropod pace. Only once does the *(expletive deleted)* driver of a sleek racing boat come too close too fast and threaten to swamp us with his wake. Luckily, all three of us stern paddlers know enough to head obliquely across the wake in order not to be caught rocking broadside in the wake's trough. We've been on the water only a few minutes when the rain begins again, lightly. I am exerting sufficiently to stay moist (and warm) as much from perspiration as from raindrops and do not bother groping in my duffel for rain gear.

Bob seems to be getting along well in spite of having a merely ceremonial paddling partner. It is clear, too, that both Monique in the bow and John in the stern are experienced canoers. In fact, a couple of times I feel obliged to ask John to adapt his pace to that of the group; he and Monique are constantly in danger, it seems, of outdistancing the rest of us. My boat is the slow one; I am not particularly powerful; and Carol, though trying to follow my technical suggestions, possesses more effervescent good humor than power or finesse.

We come to a break in the marshy island to our left. A ferry chugs past the opening, but I signal to the others to turn left and follow the less traveled way. Our boats have a shallower draft, need no deep channel and are perhaps safer out of the ferries' path. After crossing a patch of open water, we pass between two points of marsh and find ourselves in a very broad channel marked by buoys. It has started raining again, and the wind is blowing directly in our faces, making it hard both to see and to make headway. Furthermore, the tide has now turned, and though it is perhaps not yet at full flood, is trying to push us back to our launching place. Carol is tiring and needs encouragement. I am tiring and, in addition, am frustrated with my fellow travelers. Both Bob and John are having difficulty but are coping better than I am; they seem more and more likely to slip out of range of effective communication and thus become of no use to me or each other in the event of an emergency. As the person responsible for everyone's safety and welfare, I cannot tolerate this state of affairs.

Both wind and current are now directly from the north. We attempt a northwesterly course, but the wind and tide are pushing us constantly into the line of marsh grass on our left. We are all getting tired, I can see, and we are in danger of becoming separated because of the differences in personal strength, skill and stamina. It is time for drastic action. I blow my whistle, indicating that we need to stop, rest and confer.

We gather at a post marking the channel. Staying still isn't easy. The wind wants to push us into the marsh grass. But consultation, even under less than ideal conditions, is imperative.

"John," I say, when we are all together, "why does the Sierra Club go to the wilderness in *groups*?

He looks at me.

"For safety in numbers," Bob says.

"And how safe are we when we're scattered and can't communicate?"

"Not very safe," says Carol.

"If you get so far away that you can't help Erica — or me — why should I continue to feel responsible for you? In other words, why should I continue to consider you a part of this outing?"

He says nothing.

"If I have to remind you again — if I have to use my whistle — I'll ask you to leave the group."

Everyone looks uncomfortable. I am uncomfortable myself. I change the subject.

"I know we're all tired from fighting this wind and the incoming tide. I'm tired myself. I'm sorry things turned out this way; that wasn't in the plan. The good news is that when we get to the island, we'll have plenty of opportunities to relax. But right now we have to keep pulling strongly until we reach the island. We have no other choice."

It isn't bad after that. The wind blows; the tide runs, but we buffet both with renewed strength; and we stay together. Close to the ferry landing, the channel narrows, giving some relief from the wind but none from the tide. With the landing in view, our strokes gain in ease and strength.

Bear Island isn't exactly wilderness any more, since the establishment of the park and the ensuing development. We arrive at the dock beside the ferry landing, near which is a picnic shelter flanked by two enclosed toilet buildings. A road leads to a two-story bath house on the beach. Another drive branches off to the right leading to two other structures: rangers' residences. But these are the only structures on the island. The three campgrounds, one just to the south of the bathhouse and one each at the southern and northern extremes, are primitive, without facilities.

On impulse, I decide to leave my rucksack at the picnic shelter near the ferry landing and help Erica and Carol carry their gear. Why set up a tent, since it is no longer raining? Indeed, with shelters available, why set up a tent at all? (Answer: a sign prohibits overnight use of picnic shelters.)

After setting up camp and eating lunch, we meet the ranger for a talk on wildlife, notably sea turtles. He shows us places where eggs are known to be buried. These are protected from egg-loving predators—especially foxes and raccoons — by a square of steel mesh laid over the spot to discourage digging.

A notable event of the afternoon is John's capture of a Portuguese Man-of-War (genus *Physalia*) in a garbage can lid borrowed from the picnic shelter. The photograph which Monique sent me later shows its pink-and-dusky-purple sac and inky black tentacles spread ignominiously flat in the shallow water of the lid instead of floating boldly perpendicular in search of food like the illustration in my dictionary.

We swim. We have dinner. I leave the group and walk back to the ferry landing. The last ferry departs. I spend the night in a place which I am not ready to divulge. It rains, and my tent is wet on Sunday morning.

We eat. We swim. We gather for a group photograph. We eat. We swim.

The trip back is uneventful, with little wind, no rain and an incoming tide. To relieve Bob I suggest that Monique and Erica trade places, John being skillful enough to compensate for Erica's unique paddling style. A photograph shows the two of them leaving the dock. They're paddling on the same side of John's boat, the right side. Erica's right hand is fully twelve inches above the blade of the paddle, her left hand at least eight inches from the "T" grip at the end of the handle. ❖

— EIGHT - AFLOAT —
DUALITIES DOWN EAST

— EIGHT - AFLOAT —

Dualities Down East

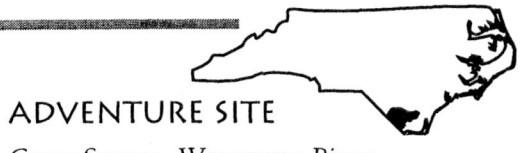

ADVENTURE SITE
*Green Swamp, Waccamaw River
North Carolina*

You can find adventure any time you step outdoors. You don't have to be at the beach or in the mountains. On the coastal plains of North Carolina there are riches awaiting any seeker whose eyes have been opened.

To appreciate some of these riches, it is often helpful to have along a scholar or two with special knowledge of natural science. Fortunately, such folk have always flocked to the Sierra Club in significant numbers: working professionals or graduate students who are willing (though sometimes it takes a bit of persuading) to share what they know.

✧

The adventure I am about to relate is enriched by the participation of several biologists. Our trip is to be a two-day affair in the vicinity of Lake Waccamaw, in southeastern North Carolina. Abby, a busy and knowledgeable botanist, is co-leading the trip with me. She has suggested the outing and agreed to lead if I'll handle publicity, recruitment and other administrative details. She has gone far beyond a mere advisory capacity; she has supplied me with information about the areas we will visit, and she has even arranged for the group's overnight accommodation with friends of hers who own a lodge on Lake Waccamaw. These friends, with whom she has stayed in the past while doing research in the area, are prepared to provide hospitality to us Sierra Club members because of our presumed scientific bent and the value of our studies to the world at large.

Of the other four biologists in the group, three are of the botanical persuasion and one of the zoological. Vonda is working on a series of Club pamphlets studying Durham county's population growth and its effect on the area's ecology. Becky is staff biologist for the state parks department. Paul is a forest ecologist interested, among other things, in the effects of acid rain in the Carolina mountains. Gerald is our sole professional zoologist. His specialties are ichthyology (see above, **Trip Four - Afloat**) and herpetology (read on).

These Club members' participation is of immense value in helping the rest of us get the most out of the week-end trip.

We are to visit the Green Swamp on the first day, stay overnight with Abby's friends and then float the Waccamaw River on Day Two.

Admittedly, mid-summer is not the ideal time to be visiting this part of Carolina. It is hot. But don't worry about us. Our group knows how to cope with the heat. You'll see.

The Green Swamp was formerly far more extensive than it is today. Like most swamps anywhere, it has been vulnerable to the desire of some to drain and cultivate it, with resulting loss of vast areas and of specialized habitats. Too bad, too, for the swamp, characterized not (like Pogo Country) by lots of water and Spanish moss but by shallow, well-burnt-over areas of pine and low plants, provides habitat for rare carnivorous plants such as the pitcher plant (Family *Sarraceniaceae*) and the Venus fly-trap *(Dionaea muscipula),* as well as other rare species.

We peer down the "throat" of the pitcher plant, where it digests the insects that fall into its deep pool of gastric juices. We watch Abby give two taps with her pencil on the tiny claw-like maw of the Venus fly-trap, which closes in response.

Our overnight stay on Lake Waccamaw is an *indoor* social adventure: cooperative cooking and convivial eating of a good spaghetti dinner.

In order to be included in this part of the book, an adventure must involve water. Fear not. On Day Two we launch our boats on the muddy Waccamaw River.

For years, while crossing the Waccamaw on our way to the Atlantic beaches, I have subjected the family to my rendition of that familiar song "Waccamaw Soul in the Bosom of Abraham." But I have never floated on it. Now comes my chance. We put in where the river flows out of broad Waccamaw Lake.

We are not facing ocean waves, whitewater rapids or other thrills. This is a muddy, narrow, slowly-winding, mosquito-ridden river of the coastal plain. We paddle between high, naked clay banks, perspiring even though our easy strokes are merely navigational, just enough to keep us off the banks and afloat in the barely discernible current. Aside from occasional briefings from the botanists in our five-boat flotilla of canoes, there is little talk until Gerald, our herpetologist, reaches his hand down and picks up something out of the muddy water.

There is immediate excitement. During this flurry, the question that occurs to me is: "How in the name of Mother Nature did Gerald ever *notice* anything in the murky element; much less *identify* it as harmless to his health and welfare?" The snake must have been swimming, as I have often seen them do, with its head above the surface. Still, Gerald's eye was sharp to spot the slim creature not more than a foot long.

"How do you know it's not poisonous?" Gerald's partner wants to know, as Gerald, having put down his paddle, is making his hands into a highway for the snake to travel.

"Because there's only one poisonous snake in this hemisphere, and this one ain't it."

"What is it?"

Gerald rattles off the common and the scientific name, but I am too far away to hear.

Soon the five boats in the flotilla are clustered around Gerald's — but not *too* near — and we are all admiring Gerald's skilled and fearless handling of the reddish-brown creature. The snake, after his or her natural manner, is eager to be on the move; therefore Gerald continually places one hand in front of the snake while holding the main bulk of the snake's length in the other hand. He makes it look easy. but it is plain that there is a knack to it that he's developed after long practice.

Remember, now, that the group is dominated by biologists of the *botanical*, not the *zoological* persuasion. The botanists as well as the non-scientists among us are in awe of Gerald's skill and daring — and not eager to rival it. Paul is the first volunteer and, after almost dropping it overboard during the transfer from Gerald's hands to his, does a fair job of providing the creature hand ahead of hand to travel on. After a brief demonstration, he is willing to hand the snake back to Gerald — this time more skillfully.

Gerald is eager to give the lady botanists lessons in snake handling. They are not enthusiastic.

"Ah, come on."

Abby finally volunteers; she's willing to try anything. But she has trouble timing the movement of her hands to match the snake's rapid pace. The other botanists have a go and, after initial awkwardness, finally get the "hang" of it, especially Becky. Some of the non-biologists are also brave enough to try. I am not brave. My "Live and help live" philosophy will most likely never require me to take up snake handling.

After Gerald drops the snake back into the muddy river, we continue on our leisurely, winding way, sweating as we go in spite of the meager effort we are putting forth. The sun is hot, and the high banks are sheltering us from any breeze that may be blowing.

"Let's stop for a swim," someone suggests as we arrive at a wide place in the river, where the banks slope gently down to the water's edge. We beach and scatter to find makeshift outdoor changing rooms.

The trip announcement, in anticipation of swimming weather, has invited participants to bring their bathing suits, and everyone has brought one — everyone but my partner Vonda, who has been occupying the bow of my canoe while I handle the stern. Everyone but her now sheds outer clothes to emerge in a swimming costume; and soon she is sitting alone on the bank while the rest of us pretend to be enjoying our swim in the muddy river.

"Come on in!" Gerald calls.

"I don't have a swim suit," she says.

"Swim without it," someone shouts.

Swimming-party humor ensues, but Vonda's only compromise is to remove her blouse and sit there in bra and shorts, hugging her knees and looking harried, hot and envious of the rest of us.

"It's muddy but cool," says one young woman.

"Yeah. Not bad."

But Vonda sits respecting the distinction society makes between women's upper-body swimwear and women's upper-body everyday support; and continues to decline. Much as she seems to want to, she can't seem to bring herself to swim in her underwear.

Now I am a great believer, like the poet Walt Whitman, in the democratic removal of all artificial barriers between persons. And, as co-organizer of the outing, it is my role to encourage full and equal participation on the part of all — especially my paddling partner.

"So okay," I say to myself. I climb out of the water, tear off my swimming trunks and jump back into the water, calling on Vonda to do the same.

In an instant everyone in the water has followed my example.

"Now *that's* leadership," I modestly mutter to myself as the other swimmers, male and female, divest and lay their suits on the bank or in their boats as if they were votive offerings to some Nature Deity.

Vonda, moved from her shyness by this spontaneous and democratic gesture, likewise gets naked and plunges into the muddy water. At first everyone is shy and uncomfortable, but soon we are all having a relaxed and joyful frolic. As we cavort in the water, the strangeness seems to fall away. Are we responding to the Ultimate Democracy? Or leaping eons back — to an Edenic innocence?

So comfortable, in fact, do we become that it is not easy to get anyone to dress again. The day isn't getting any cooler; and now something has transformed the atmosphere of the outing. Most of us get back into the boats without donning our clothes. Our social inhibitions have been, if not put aside, at least temporarily abated. At the same time, one's otherwise unsatisfied curiosity about the anatomies of our fellow Club members can now be satisfied, so long as one ogles discreetly. As we continue down the winding river, some of my fellow Club members' secrets are revealed with no one missing a paddle stroke: the impressive male members of some of my fellow male members: the astounding buxomness of our skinniest colleague; the anatomical perfection of our most unassuming cohort; and one friend's episiotomy scar. I am struck by the physical diversity of my colleagues as well as their sudden willingness to reveal themselves in the Great Outdoors.

"We're getting close to civilization" Abby warns. She does not make a move to reclothe herself. But soon we begin to see houses set back in the bankside trees. Reluctantly, one by one, the paddlers don their garments.

❖

Needless to say, it was a memorable trip. I learned, and am sure the other participants learned, more than expected, not only about the wild creation but also about each other's capacity for raw, elemental decency, given the least encouragement.

And — oh, yes — about the dualities promised in this **Trip's** title:

- swamp — river
- scientist — non-scientist
- botanist — zoologist
- land — water
- prepared — unprepared
- plant carnivores — generous human beings
- fear of snakes — snake handling
- clothed — naked

Are those enough dualities for one wilderness adventure? ❖

—NINE - AFLOAT—
The Dan at Flood

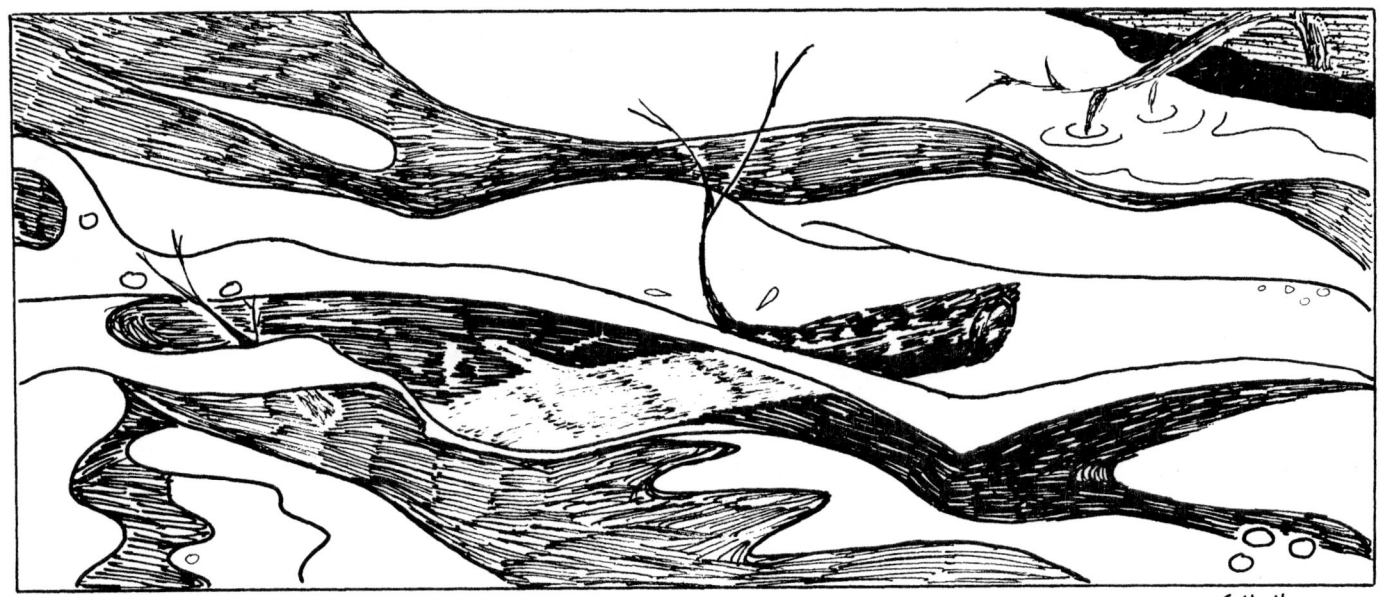

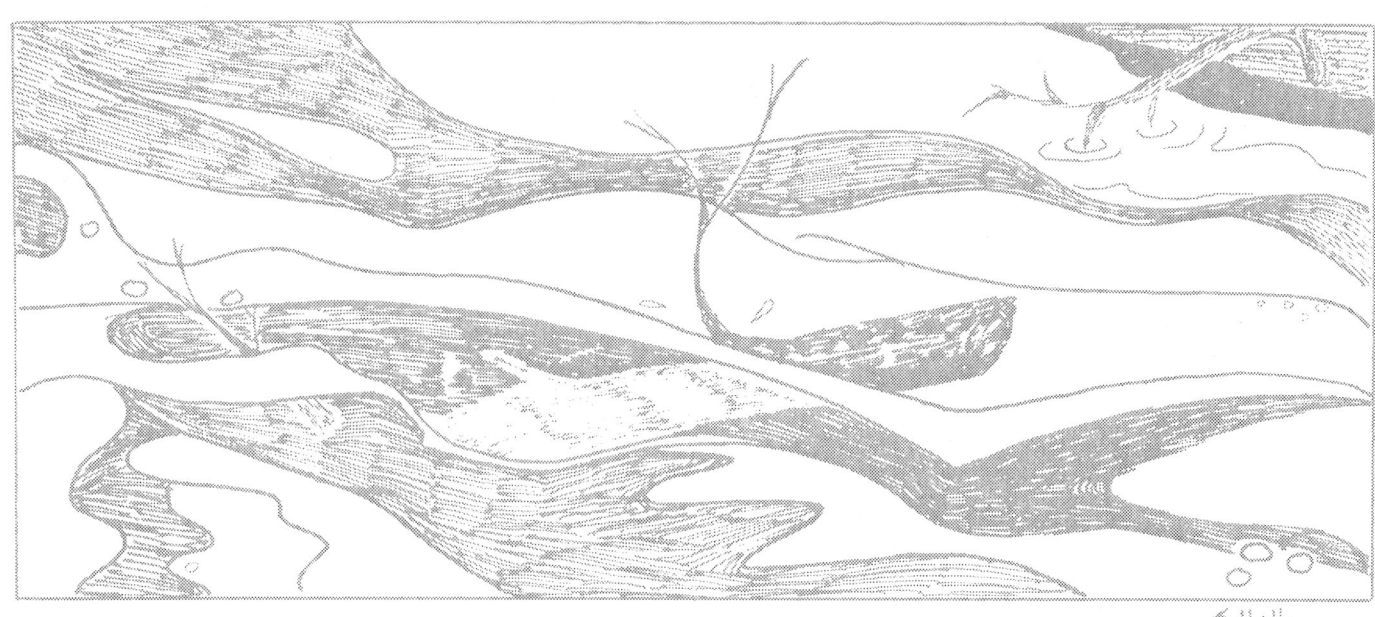

— NINE - AFLOAT —
THE DAN AT FLOOD

ADVENTURE SITE

*Dan River, Stokes County
North Carolina*

I spent the week-end of June 16-18, 1989 paddling on the Dan River between Francisco and Danbury, camping at Hanging Rock State Park. I'd paddled that part of the river before, *but not in flood time.*

It had rained each day the previous week, and it rained for several hours on Friday evening as I drove to the park, David following in his van with his family's Grumman aluminum canoe strapped on top.

❖

As the roads cross and re-cross the Dan, it becomes clear to me that this is not the Dan I've known. This one is muddier and mightier, swifter and more swollen. Passing through Danbury, I turn right off Sheppard Mill Road and pull into the parking area at Moratock Park. Dave pulls in beside me.

"What's up?"

"I want to look at my 'gauge rock.'"

"Gauge rock?" He swings shut the van door and follows me across the parking lot.

"There's a Class 1 rapid right at the head of this horseshoe bend, just before it starts around the park."

"So?"

"When it's up so high I can tell what kind of run we'll have." We have arrived at the edge of the parking lot and step from it to the river bank. "Holy cow!"

"What's the matter?"

"There's no rapid there; never mind the 'gauge rock.' You can't see *any* rocks. That rapid has been wiped out completely. It's drowned. This is going to be SOME TRIP !"

Dave isn't sure what to make of this observation; he's new to the Dan River but an old hand at river paddling — *he says.* You can't prove it by me; I've never paddled with him before.

I am not totally unprepared for this trip. I know that David's aluminum boat will be slower than my sleek A.B.S. plastic Mohawk and that, being keeled, it will be harder to turn. What I don't know is David's skill or his level of bravado, though I have had hints of the latter from his sister, who refuses to paddle with him. I don't know what new access structures have been added to the canoe trail since my last visit. I don't know how soon it will stop raining or, if it does, how rapidly the water will subside. I have no clear idea of how the volume, swiftness and turbidity of the water will affect our ability to "read" the river and maneuver in it.

The camp ground at Hanging Rock State Park, amazingly, is almost full. We find a site on the edge of things, the last site as Circle 2 enters the main drive. Here we should be away from the noise, since we are as far as possible from the bath house; nevertheless we are entertained by the sound of hilarity and loud applause from a big group of campers until long after the start of posted quiet hours. I would be content with merely the sound of the wind in the trees and the rain on the tent-top and, after the rain stops, the thin little sound of crickets.

The shuttle Saturday is easy. We leave my truck at the new landing steps upstream from NC Highway 89 bridge and drive to Francisco in Dave's van. Dave has a question.

"What's this section like?"

"Shallow and scrapey — usually. If it hasn't been raining, there are sections where you sometimes end up walking and dragging the boat."

"Shouldn't be a problem today."

"Nope. Today we should have lovely, continuous Class 2 rapids."

"Any tough ones?"

"I used to think Lunch Stop Rapid was pretty tricky. All the water has to make a sweep around a rock that's undercut. No telling how the high water will affect it today."

We have decided that because of the swiftness of the current, we'll be able to paddle two sections in one day. Each of these is considered a day's trip. We park on the road shoulder river left and carry boat and gear to the launching place under the bridge. When we have tied gear into the boat, I glance at my watch. Nine-thirty. Water is rushing past the bridge piers more rapidly than I have ever seen it here; there is more of it, and it is muddier.

"Might be hard to see the rocks today," Dave says.

"Yep."

"This is a nice eddy for launching."

"True. Only problem may be getting the boat turned in time to run the first rapids."

"How about if we point the bow downstream?"

"Okay," I say, still not sure what kind of paddler Dave is. But if he thinks he can handle the stern —

Dave, a gentleman, holds the boat while I mount. I, in turn, plant my paddle in the soft bank until Dave says "Go!" giving the boat a shove out into the center of the narrow river and quickly ruddering to line up for the first small rapid. Frankly, I am surprised not to see rocks mid-river here; I seem to remember flat rocks close to the surface just below the put-in that usually make the shallow channel hard to find. Not to worry, today. We float down the center, with no scraping on the usually-scrapey mid-river rocks.

Not to worry at all, we soon conclude. There's plenty of depth for Dave's boat or, when we scrape, enough river velocity to pull us forward. It is a relief not to have to worry much about finding a deep enough channel in this sometimes-shallow section of the river. "Go with the flow." Still David, paddling in the stern and proving to be a better paddler than I have any right to expect, often dismounts to push the boat off rocks. I can't help thinking we'd be better off in my keelless plastic boat. But Dave is great; he doesn't hesitate. Sometimes I have the impression we could easily get free of a snag by rocking the boat in unison, but Dave, at the slightest bump or scrape, bounds out of the boat in his wet tennis shoes, wading and tugging to free the boat. After a while I resign myself to letting Dave "do his thing." I stay in the boat and try to balance while scoping a route through any remaining rock garden. Lunch Stop Rapid proves to be no great challenge; the river's flow carries us through even the maze of rock garden upstream from the chute with more force on its part than exercise of skill on ours. Almost, it seems, before we've started down this beautiful, remote section of the river, we glance up and spy NC 704 bridge. There is no hint of the shoals by Riverside Park. It is early, but we decide to stop for lunch.

I have put in and taken out several times before at Riverside Park but have never met the owner. This time, though, we are in luck: Mr. Tucker is hanging out at the pavilion of the former dance hall and has the door open so that we can peek inside. After our brief inspection he warmly encourages us to use the patio as a lunching place. Dave, a gregarious fellow who hasn't brought much lunch, draws out Mr. Tucker while I crunch my carrot and munch my mozzarella sandwich. One thing we learn from our host, aside from his personal and a lot of local history, is that the canoe trail's new landing is just downstream from the bridge, on river left. This, then, may be the last time I'll ever beach at Riverside Park.

Back on the river, we make another quick, short trip, taking out at NC 89 bridge at 2:30. Landing is a sociable and exciting experience, for two groups of paddlers are winding up their trips there at the same time. One group is aborting its outing, which has started right here, because one of its three boats has been flung broadside into the pile of flotsam resting against the middle bridge pier, and has overturned and become so tightly snared and heavy with water that a tow truck has been called to draw it out of the river. Most of the excitement has subsided by the time we arrive; the boats have been loaded onto a van and are in the process of being tied down.

The other group of paddlers is a Sierra Club group led by my old river pal Allen Trelease. I've known he was going to be on the river this day and have half-suspected that we might encounter him, as I did on the section last year. That time my group met his by prearrangement at the put-in and traveled downriver under his expert leadership. Section 3, which we've paddled this morning, is Allen's favorite section of the river. We've also, because of the super-swiftness of the river, completed Section 4. Section 5, which starts here, is twelve miles long.

While I am socializing with Allen and other acquaintances in the group, a sharp-eyed amateur archaeologist in the aborting group, sauntering down a couple of rows in the neighboring cornfield, bends down and picks up a 3000-year-old arrowhead; or maybe a spear point; I don't get a good look at it.

Even after all the socializing, it is early when Dave and I arrive back at the campground. We could have done <u>three</u> sections in one day! What a difference water level makes! We hike to the summit of Hanging Rock Mountain. Dave goes for a swim. I go to bed early.

By Sunday morning the water is drastically down from its Friday evening level. The rapid at Moratock, which we carefully study after parking Dave's van at the trail access, looks a lot like its old self, rocks now evident and two clear choices of channel. Four other canoers are parking their shuttle vehicle. We meet them again and chat with them as we put in at 89 bridge.

❖

The section from 89 bridge to Moratock Park is a less dramatic whitewater experience than the one afforded by the two sections upstream. At the same time, it is scenic, pastoral and relaxing. We do have one challenge at the start. You remember the debris against the bridge piers? Studying it as we put in, we can see that it is spread across nearly the entire width of the river (which in fact isn't very broad at this point) so that the only clear passage requires a sharp turn toward the left bank and then a sharp right turn under the left span of the bridge.

After meeting this challenge, we settle into a routine. Our roles have changed, for now I am in the stern. I'm happy to say that even in the aluminum canoe and in spite of the many places where the river is quite broad and shallow, we get stuck only once, and I'm not convinced Dave needs to hop out as spryly and promptly as he does. The current is markedly slower than yesterday, and we have leisure for wildlife observation. David knows a lot about birds, has brought his binoculars with him and can identify the red-eyed vireo (*Vireo olivaceus*), the peewee (*Cantopus virens*) and many other birds by their calls. At one point we see a congregation of kingfishers (*Megaceryle alcyon*), a dozen or more, more than I've ever seen together of this usually solitary species. We speak of the wood thrush's (*Hylocichla mustelina's*) characteristic broken arpeggios, the many hemlocks (*tsuga*) along the shore (Dave isn't very familiar with these) and the dominance of willow (*salix*) and river birch (*Betula nigra*). I introduce Dave to the spiderwort (*Tradescantia virginiana*), which we see in significant numbers along the banks; I mention its reputed radiation-detecting capability. A merganser mama (*Lophodytes cucullatus*), she of the loose, tawny crest and spikelike bill, bursts into the canoe's path and half-swims, half-flies through the water for half a mile, leading us along with the old broken-wing deception downstream and presumably away from her hidden brood of ducklings before flying back upstream. We enjoy the moss-covered cliffs, the clear blue sky.

We beach and lunch at the new access at Indian River and, wishing we had a copy of the Stokes County Recreation map for orientation, sample a short stretch of the Mountains-to-Sea Trail. I find it isn't great fun to hike in wet neoprene boots with water squishing around in them.

Some time during the day we get to thinking about how much fun teenagers would have mastering the river and even hearing two enthusiastic nature-lovers rhapsodizing about saving the planet. We encounter fishermen and tubers but no other paddlers until Moratock Park, where Dave has sufficient free attention while running Horseshoe Rapid to look toward the parking lot and identify the four canoeists we've seen in the morning. They've made the trip in two hours; it has taken Dave and me three (you see the difference between an aluminum hull and a plastic one?) Or maybe it's the difference between serious gawkers and serious paddlers.

Still, for a mostly flat-water trip, that's fast. I don't expect I'll travel that fast again on the Dan River.

❖

Days after our trip we hear that officials have been using the local radio to warn people off the "raging river." Not being local, we were unaware of the warnings. No doubt there were reasons for the caution, particularly for beginners: floating trees and other debris; swift current with resulting need for hair-trigger maneuvering. But Dave and I have not felt unduly challenged. Saturday's trip was more enjoyable at high water than it would have been at low; and by Sunday much of the flood's excitement was "water under the bridges" of Stokes County. ❖

— TEN - AFLOAT —
FOLLOWING THE HOLY CROSS

— TEN - AFLOAT —
Following the Holy Cross

ADVENTURE SITE
*St. Croix River,
Border Maine &
New Brunswick, Canada*

It is a wonderfully clear day in Vanceboro, Maine. At just past noon the temperature has already climbed to 90 degrees. Lea and I are standing amongst bits and bundles of scattered gear in a field between the General Store and the St. Croix River having a stand-up lunch, listening to the turbulence of "Kill-Me-Quick Rips" and wondering whether we can pack all this gear in a way that will get it through the turbulence without a spill and a soaking. As we look upstream, we can see cars crossing the bridge between Maine, U.S.A., and New Brunswick Province, Canada.

During weeks of preparation (maps; guides; camping gear; modifications to my beat-up green Mohawk canoe; vehicle-swapping (for gasoline economy); and during other adventures in Maine, what we have been most anticipating is our launch on the St. Croix, along the Maine-Canada border.

Because the St. Croix, like most east-coast rivers, flows southerly; and because it is always a good idea to scout the take-out before putting in, if only to recognize it from the river, we decide to stop at Loon Bay on our way to Vanceboro. According to all the maps and guides, the short-cut to Loon Bay from the south is the Bingo Road, off U.S. 1. Bingo is categorized in The Maine Atlas (published by DeLorme Mapping) under the heading "Other Improved Roads" but looks to us better than its description. That's because instead of turning left onto a gravel road, we continue on the lumpy, pot-holed pavement, which soon degrades into dirt track, probably a logging road: overgrown, blocked with branches; beset with muddy pools; devoid of landmarks and calculated to lose both us and the hours we've "gained" by rising before dawn. In the end we seem to have little choice but to retrace to U.S. 1 and head north to another road, better marked and partly paralleling the river. We find our take-out, Loon Bay, a beautiful spot boasting a primitive campground and a sportsman's lodge.

❖

Just after mid-day we arrive in Vanceboro, which to us city folks seems not much of a town: customs station, bridge to Canada, general store. The Great Unknown is how to arrange a shuttle.

"Oh, my husband does that after hours," says the clerk in the General Store. "Just load up your boat and bring us your key. We'll take your truck to Loon Bay after closing tonight or tomorrow morning. We'll hide the key, and the truck will be there when you arrive at Loon Bay tomorrow evening."

Behind the store, we walk to the river.

"Wow! What a put-in! What a wild put-in!"

"Kill-Me-Quick Rips" is 100 yards of foot-high boiling waves, no doubt indicating the presence of big, stream-rounded underwater rocks. The river, the clerk in the General Store told us, is rain-swollen. Not much danger, she said, of hitting rocks. But to us it looks as if there will be plenty of chance of taking water over the gunwales.

And there's another problem we'll have to face immediately. Only a few feet downstream from the put-in is a huge boulder against the near bank. We'll have to head quickly toward the center of the swift, 15-foot-wide river, but not so quickly that we'll get broadside to the current and start taking on water.

I hold the boat. Lea steps in.

"Paddle on the left, and draw immediately. We have to miss the rock, but we don't want to turn too sharply and present too much hull to the current; Kill-Me-Quick Rips could kill us quick."

I step into the stern, kneel quickly, and push the stern away from the bank as Lea performs a draw stroke to pull the bow away. As soon as there's space for it, I make one sweep stroke, which provides enough angle to get us past the rock.

"Now paddle!" I shout, for we are in the center of the river, amidst the turbulence of the standing waves. We are taking on water in little splashes, not in dangerous amounts. The rips continue with diminishing ferocity for half a mile, to a bridge, the last bridge we'll see on the trip. We have of course brought along bailer and sponge and, in the smoother water below the rips, we have time for housekeeping. We settle in for a peaceful day on the river. Though we have put in at 2:00 p.m. rather than 9:00 as planned, we seem to have plenty of time to get where we are going. Of course, never having been there before, we're not quite sure *where* we're going, but we are in a humor to feel we have "all the time in the world." The storekeeper has told us that there was a race last week: the best time Vanceboro to Loon Bay was something like two hours and eleven minutes. We have allotted two days.

Plenty of time to enjoy each other's company or to be alone with one's thoughts. No need to talk.

Yet we aren't always alone on the river. Others are enjoying it, too, usually not in groups, but in pairs or singly. Each time we call out to ask advice about how to run the next rapid, we get a prompt and helpful reply. This promptness is important in view of the swiftness of the current (remember that it's been raining upstream) and the speed with which we approach and pass other paddlers, some sitting still and some even paddling upstream. Usually we get more help than we ask for, and most of the extra advice has to do with Little Falls, the mid-point of the twenty-mile trip and its most thrilling rapid. We begin to develop a quite specific Little Falls phobia.

All paddling is work. On the St. Croix, at least in the first part of the run, rapids are frequent. On smooth water, one may feel safe and comfortable sitting on the seat. In running a rapid, one wishes to lower the center of gravity (and minimize the danger of capsizing) by kneeling in the bilge. Just getting down to kneel for each rapid and getting back up on the seat again afterwards is providing a bit of a work-out.

When the river is broad and smooth, we chat; we consult compass and guide-book; we loaf; we watch the clear water and the movement of puffy cumulus clouds in the perspicuous blue; the floating ducks; the flying hawks, ospreys and eagles; only an occasional jumping fish or sunning tortoise. We haven't been reading newspapers, and the world seems far away. Maine's "Life in the Slow Lane" is beginning to agree with us.

There are moments of risk, as befits even the mildest adventure. Since we have scorned the detailed but overpriced maps for sale in Vanceboro, we aren't always clear which way the often serpentine river will curve or which is the main channel. The river often widens into broad, grassy coves which threaten to draw us in. We hope we are keeping to the main flow, but sometimes it's hard to identify.

We are on the look-out for a likely-looking camping place.

"How about that place?" Lea is pointing with her paddle.

"Looks good to me."

It is a peninsula on river right, downstream from a broad and tempting backwater, upstream from what looks like a tributary stream. There's only one drawback: the flat and attractive-looking camping area is atop a bank two feet above the water. Dismounting is a cooperative, one-at-a-time effort. Likewise the unloading.

But there's this advantage: a sudden rise in water level won't drown us — unless it's super-monstrous.

Setting up camp is routine; we've been doing it at least every other night for a week and have mastered the steps. Soon we have the bedding inside the tent, the supper things cleared away and extra stuff protected as well as can be under the overturned canoe. It's time for fun and games: home entertainment 900 miles from home. Lea finds an eagle feather and, wearing it in her hair, sanctifies our new stomping ground with a special ceremonial stomp. We explore our new environs. We sleep serenaded by the rolling river, dreaming of Little Falls, still unknown and yet to come.

Next morning after breakfast I perform another ritual in order to benefit some trees and the next visitors to this spot. I disperse a fire ring, which has been damaging shallow tree roots and generally diminishing the wilderness experience for anyone stopping here.

We have not been long on the river when we begin to hear the sound of rapids — louder sounds of friction between water and rock than we have heard thus far on the trip. Little Falls? The question is answered when the river horizon downstream becomes a hard line beyond which we cannot see.

The right bank seems to afford a beaching and scouting place. We land, look and listen for ten or fifteen minutes, walking individually up and down the bank paying more attention to the river than to each other. Then, with hardly any discussion, we decide to run the more challenging Class 3 near side instead of doing a long upstream ferry to the easier-looking Class 2 "sneak" route opposite. Either option culminates in fifty yards of rip downstream. Having opted for the four-foot drop, we need to choose a path over it and into the churning rips below. Lea, a paddler less than a year, has never attempted anything like it, and I applaud her choice. I have attempted one or two Class 3 rapids (for example, Penitentiary and Molly Shoals on the New River), but not without swimming involuntarily.

We agree on what appears to be the "best" channel on river right. Here there seems to be enough water pouring over the lip to carry the boat and its piles of gear. Unfortunately, just at the place where the bow will strike as it clears the ledge, there is a sizable rock smack in the center of the channel. Is there enough water splashing up from this rounded rock to float the bow, and then the stern? I don't feel completely confident.

We've been told by a river guidebook that most paddlers portage gear around Little Falls in order to lighten boats before running.

"To heck with that. Untying and retying all that gear? Too much trouble!"

I feel a little worried that there may be pin-holes in some of the garbage bags containing our stuff, but why have we double-bagged and tied everything securely if not to protect it in just such a situation as this?

We are a bit intimidated. "Pump-pump" and "thump-thump" goes the old ticker in my chest as we adjust our life jackets and ferry upstream, lining to hit the drop four feet to the right of that rocky island with the small tree on it.

"Well, here goes!"

"Hey! Yippee!"

We hit the drop just right.

We even manage to miss the rock below, turning slightly to the left in order to ride the crest of the rips downstream.

Even before reaching the rips, we have taken several big waves over the bow. By the time we are halfway through the rips, the water in the bilge has reached within a hand's length of the gunwales, making the boat very hard to maneuver. We are paddling furiously in order to avoid being "pooped," submerged by water coming in over the stern. The bow is plowing through a standing wave every five feet, and each wave threatens to fill the boat beyond our ability to manage. It is futile to try to shout over the roar of the rapid, but tacitly we seem to agree it is time to head for the landing on the right to beach, dump and recoup.

"Well done!" shouts a young man on the bank as the bow grunch pad grinds to a halt in the sand. He immediately identifies himself as a river guide. Lea begins engaging him in conversation, but my attention goes first to the water in the boat and the need to dump it quickly before our bundles start leaking. Once the boat is upside down, with water pouring out of it but all of our gear staying where it's been tied, I am relieved enough to be ready for sociability.

Standing with the guide are his two charges: a young boy readying a kayak and a woman who could be his mother. The latter is watching as the guide straps down gear to D-rings in the bilge of the new-looking *Old Town* canoe.

"Have you ever run this river before?" the young man asks.

"No."

"Would you like to join us?" Something about his manner, though he is friendly enough and nonchalant enough, suggests that he may know important things about the rest of the trip that we do not — and should.

I look briefly at Lea. She seems relaxed. "No; I guess not." Perhaps we are expressing more confidence than we feel. But we are enjoying our own company and, after all, have just now negotiated the most challenging rapid on this section of the St. Croix. From here the trip should be "all downhill."

We wave Good-bye while the Guide is still strapping down gear.

"See you on the river !"

We aren't yet finished with the excitement. The roar of rapids greets us again in a moment and after that again and again. Each time we hear the sound, we kneel in anticipation.

We stop for lunch on the left bank, in Canada. We see no barriers or border guards. That feels good. The guide, the boy and the woman float by as we sit lunching. Again they invite us to join them at a shelter and picnic table just downstream, on the Canadian side, and again we politely decline. When we float by them a few minutes later, they have beached and are enjoying a dip.

Soon we thread our way through the "Grassy Islands" described in the guidebook. Below the islands we stalk and photograph a young loon (*Gavia immer*), finding it not so shy as loons are reputed to be.

We have read that the St. Croix was heavily used during the last century to float timber down to the mill. We see remnants of that use: water-logged tree-trunks submerged in fairly clear water near the banks. We have also read of the log booms placed along the channel to prevent logs from escaping into coves and slack water. The decaying of the lost and leftover logs in the St. Croix is depleting the river's oxygen, preventing the thriving of fish populations. Seeing these logs through the shallow tea-colored water, we are reminded that during the entire trip we have seen few fish jumping. We have been traveling in a dead river. [DON'T WASTE PAPER.]

All too soon we see houses on the Canadian side and recognize them as the ones we noted as we scouted the take-out. Crossing the river from the fishing camp to these houses is a power line high above the river, the first we have seen, and a sure sign of civilization. Our trip is over. We can be pleased to have tucked away some new experiences, but we leave the beautiful Holy Cross River with regret, washing our boots, stowing gear, tying down the boat and heading off again down the Bingo Road.

❖

Maybe, another day, we'll tackle another Canadian river. Each river, we have found, is unique. ❖

— ELEVEN - AFLOAT —
Suggestions For A Rainy Day

— ELEVEN - AFLOAT —
SUGGESTIONS FOR A RAINY DAY

ADVENTURE SITE
*Flat River, Durham &
Person Counties
North Carolina*

I am going to give you a suggestion about what an outdoor person might do on a rainy day. What does an adventurous person do when it's "too wet" for an outdoor adventure? I'll make my suggestion as I tell you what some of us "outdoor persons" actually did one rainy February day.

You would have to admit that the day after Valentine's 1992 was wet. On Friday, February 14th the weather man predicted an 89 percent chance of rain all day Saturday. By Saturday afternoon the forecast was changed to a 100 percent chance, with a high in the low 50s. What does an outdoor person do when the weather acts like that?

Having received much of my outdoor conditioning in the Sierra Club, which has a "Trips go rain or shine" philosophy, I do not believe in canceling a trip until I get to the trailhead and find that the weather conditions are absolutely life-threatening (for a story about Brad Bush, a Sierra Club leader who practiced that philosophy, see above, **Trip Nine - Afoot: "Comin' 'Round Mt. Rogers"**).

◆

My friend Lea enjoys canoeing at least as much as I do. Furthermore, she has, for sentimental reasons, a particular attachment to the Flat River, which the city of Durham has dammed (damned?) to form Lake Michie, part of the city's water supply. In turn, Lake Michie feeds Falls Lake, which eventually contracts to be merely the vastly polluted Neuse River.

The Flat was the first river Lea ever paddled, and when I complain that it's been a coon's age since I've wet a paddle, she casts her vote for a trip on the Flat. And since we're going, why not invite David (not the David of **Nine - Afloat**), the new outings chair of the Trail Association and a good canoeist. And if David is going, and has a tandem boat, why not invite Julie, a fellow resident of David's apartment building?

And so it is arranged.

I get up early and pack a lunch for two. While I am doing it, Lea calls.

"Are we going?"

"Sure."

"I'll bet David will call you." While I am eating breakfast, he does.

"Are we going?"

I explain my "Decide-at-the-trailhead" philosophy.

When we get to the trailhead, believe it or not, it isn't raining. I am pleased that though, not wishing to insult the intelligence of my outdoor companions, I've said nothing of cold/wet weather gear, all of them are adequately swathed in polypropylene and wool, with rain clothes, hats, gloves and footwear appropriate for muddy banks and frigid wading.

Now there's one other thing you need to know in order to appreciate this story. The Flat River, in southern Person and northern Durham counties, is a wet-weather river. Don't bother putting in unless it's been raining for a day or so. If the water level is low, depend on the rock level to be high. So paddle the Flat in winter or, at the latest, in late spring.

The first time I paddled the Flat was in late March about four years ago, leading a Sierra Club trip. I've been back three times since, and I can confirm what Bob Benner's guidebook says: the Flat is a wet-weather river.

At the trailhead, we four look at the totally overcast sky. Clearly, it will rain before long.

"Well," says David, "it's not raining now; so let's go."

We tie in gear and go.

I don't think Julie has ever paddled before (another convert baptized, like Lea, on the Flat); but she is a good sport. She laughs a lot: a high, warm and joyous note. She is a welcome recruit to the Fellowship of River Crazies, most of us sane enough in other respects but with that one inexplicable aberration: we believe that bumper sticker that says: A BAD DAY ON THE RIVER IS BETTER THAN A GOOD DAY AT WORK.

But it is a *good* day on the river. At the put-in we find an old mill, the frame building, iron works and mill race still largely intact. We see beaver signs, those unmistakable gnawed ends of limbs and several down trees stripped of bark, winter food for the family snug in the lodge. Birds twitter all day, even during downpours. We see a flying owl and three or four kinds of wild ducks swimming. There's also the challenge of boulder-dodging, channel-seeking and rock-garden wading. And the all-day, frigid drizzle, which turns into light rain at times — said to be good for the complexion!

But really, I am so warmly dressed in pile and polypropylene that I am damp more from within, perspiring, than from the rain outside.

And you may believe this or not, but my partner notices, during one rock-garden walk, pulling the boat, that the canoe's thwarts are casting shadows. I never see the sun, but she claims those shadows are proof of its presence among the clouds. Maybe so. What is more certain is that as we drive home, we witness columns of rain falling from layers of nimbus clouds against a red sunset; and as we unload our gear, the waxing gibbous moon shines through for a moment.

❖

Had I sat at home reading, would I have experienced all this?
So here's my suggestion for a rainy day: GO CANOEING!

❖

By the way, when I got home, guess what message I found on my answering machine.

No; you'll never guess; I'd better tell you.

Please remember what kind of Saturday this was.

"Hello. This is Scott T. Sauer [my son-in-law, the County Manager]. We were just calling to see what your plans are for this evening. But I guess you're out floating on the river somewhere."

Now who would expect even the County Manager to be *that* perceptive? ❖

—TWELVE - AFLOAT—
OKEFENOKEE II WITH SAMMY OLIVER

– TWELVE - AFLOAT –

OKEFENOKEE II WITH SAMMY OLIVER

ADVENTURE SITE
Okefenokee Wildlife Refuge
Georgia-Florida

A 1996 publication off the National Geographic Society features the Okefenokee National Wildlife Refuge as one of the few remaining wild places on the planet Earth. Frankly, I was surprised to see that, for I knew something of the area's history and realized that plenty of human beings have exerted themselves to rape, exploit, despoil and destroy the natural beauty of that unique place. I know that the swamp, magnificent as it is in its variety of natural terrain and wildlife, is not as natural as it used to be.

The native American tribes that inhabited the swamp as early as 2500 B.C.E. were not among its destroyers. Tribes of the "Deptford Culture," the "Swift Creek Culture" and the "Weeden Island Culture" had homes here. Even the Seminoles, the last to use the swamp as a sanctuary, lived lightly upon the Okefenokee, the "land of the trembling earth," until an armed militia led by General Charles R. Floyd drove them into Florida in 1850.

In 1891 the Suwannee Canal Company bought 238,120 acres of the swamp from the state of Georgia, intending to drain, log and eventually farm it. For three years Captain Henry Jackson's crews labored to create 11.5 miles of the Suwannee Canal, digging the company into bankruptcy in the process. The Hebard Cypress Company acquired the tract in 1899, built a railroad in from the western edge and began timbering. By 1927, when the cutting stopped, over 431,000,000 board feet of lumber had been taken out.

The Refuge was established in 1937 and now includes 396,000 acres. In 1974, the interior 353,981 acres were designated as a National Wilderness Area.

After my first visit to the Refuge, I harbored a lingering desire to go back. I soon discovered that the Okefenokee's many-splendored beauty plays a coy game of hard-to-get with the public, thanks to the Interior Department's stewardship. Balancing protection of the natural swamp ecology with the need to share with the public, the Fish and Wildlife Service has established a permitting process which makes it quite necessary to plan well in advance for an Okefenokee adventure. I began in the fall of 1987 to plan for an Easter 1988 trip into the Refuge.

For twenty cents I acquired a one-sheet, three-fold brochure with all the rules and regulations and a color-coded map. Through correspondence I learned that in order to obtain a permit for one of the 15 "Designated Canoe Trips" on the Yellow Trail, the Red Trail, the Green Trail, the Brown Trail, the Blue Trail, the Orange Trail or the Purple Trail, one makes a reservation by phone, by mail or in person. But, says the brochure, *"Reservations can be made no earlier than two months to the day in advance to* [sic] *the intended departure date."* And furthermore, "reservations made in person can only be made by the authorized trip leader."

In 1979 I traveled the Red Trail on Easter week-end, a good time to go. At this time of year one can hope for the beginnings of warm weather; and if one's luck is holding, the water level will be sufficient to keep you from getting bogged down in the ever-encroaching water-lilies on the often shallow trail cuts; and the mosquitoes will not have hatched and swarmed yet. But there's a fly in that ointment: the long Easter week-end is an attractive time not only to me but also to other adventurers; thus the competition for reservations on that particular week-end is keen.

But hope springs eternal, and on the assumption that I'd be able to get the permit when the time came, I placed a notice in *The Source,* newsletter of the Headwaters Group of the Sierra Club. It may have been the October issue. Knowing that money talks, that all other talk is cheap and that the Refuge has a daily camping fee, I asked for a non-refundable registration fee up front and sent an ecstatic description of the swamp's charms. By December 1 I was receiving checks, letters and serious inquiries, in response to which I sent out my first letter to prospective participants, enclosing in each a photocopy of the Refuge's canoe trail brochure. Since the copy was not in color, I gave the address of the Refuge and encouraged prospective adventurers to get their own copies so that they could enjoy the color-coded map of the Red Trail, the Yellow Trail, etc.

I could not, of course, guarantee that the trip would materialize, since all was contingent on getting a reservation. I had learned from previous contacts with Refuge headquarters that the office opens at 7:00 a.m., that the telephones start ringing even before that time and that the staff doesn't begin answering the telephone so long as there is someone at the door wanting to talk about a reservation. Gaining all this information has required persistent effort over the months and years between 1979 and 1987. In the light of all this, I decided to make the trip south to Georgia from my homestead near the Carolina-Virginia border in order to be one of those waiting at the office door before 7:00 a.m.

The cap of my pick-up truck makes a fine auxiliary dormitory. I had reason to know some of the out-of-the-way parking (read "hiding") places in the area surrounding the Refuge, and my alarm clock was working well enough that I was on hand not only before the office opened but early enough to witness the arrival, while it was still dark, of my principal competitor for the pick of canoe trips for the following Easter week-end. In fact, I still have his business card. He made the trip from Atlanta in order to further his own tradition of taking his friends into the Refuge on Easter week-end each year.

During my permit-scouting trip I did some hiking among the alligators, deer, red-seeded bay trees and brown cypress knees; I groped in the early morning fog, heard the call of the barred owl and the pileated woodpecker; felt rain so fine it seemed a mere mist; felt the caress of the warm morning breezes and inhaled the disturbing fragrance of newly-burned stands of pine outside the Refuge. I acquired information about the Okefenokee Swamp Park, a commercial venture which penetrates the Refuge's northern border.

On my birthday in February of 1988 I wrote my second letter to trip participants, a three-pager which, among other things, reported:

> *It's ours! A permit for the best canoe trip of those offered: most popular, hardest to get, the one I've experienced, years back: the arc from Kingfisher Landing to Stephen Foster Park (Florida) by way of Maul Hammock and Big Water Lake. A fabulous trip, full of pleasant memories for me. I'm curious to see whether it will be fun for a group as big as ours promises to be.*

My letter listed the names, addresses and telephone numbers of the sixteen participants, coded to suggest canoeing partners; listed equipment requirements; gave road directions; summarized pertinent Refuge rules and described arrangements for using the chemical toilet which all parties must carry along.

I closed with this peroration:

> *I know all of us are planning this trip at least in part to let the natural order of things flow through us, not to inflict anything of ourselves on it, whether of material leavings or unduly polluting sounds. Therefore we will of course study to be so far as humanly feasible in still harmony with one another and with the Spirit of the Place which the Seminoles called "The Land of Trembling Earth."*

One more letter, dated March 21, went out to trip participants:

Subject: "Tent-a-tiff" Sleeping Platform Arrangements and other odds and ends

Believe it or not, I have been spending time making scale drawings of the 22-foot x 28-foot camping platforms on the Okefenokee canoe trails and, try as I may, I find no better arrangement (leaving space for the wind to blow in at the open sides) than to put six tents in three rows of two in one direction (lengthwise) or three rows of two in the other (lengthwise).

In either case, we end up with six SIX — count 'em — SIX tents for 16 persons on the trip listed above (count 'em). As you know, sixteen persons distributed in six tents comes to 2.6666666 persons per tent. It seems convenient not to divide families, relationships or persons in planning sleeping arrangements. Therefore I propose an arrangement resembling that on the following page [which contains a diagram]. The primary purpose of the tents, frankly (barring rain) is to separate persons from mosquitoes and the raccoons.

I poke my big camel's nose into the tent arrangements for this reason: if I don't — if we don't give some thought to the matter and either follow my suggestion or an alternative offered before departure time — there's a risk of not taking along a sufficient number of free-standing tents that will accommodate the required two or three persons. Right? Thus my proposal. What is your thought? If you like my arrangement, then one of the sleep-mates needs to find a sufficiently roomy free-standing tent, get it in shape, learn how to erect it and see that it gets loaded and carried to Kingfisher Landing. I don't own a free-standing tent; that is, one that can be erected on a wooden platform without driving nails. I hope someone in each group has one that will serve or can borrow one. We will of course need "regular" tents for camping at Stephen Foster Park. Planning ahead, we may be able to avoid unnecessary packing, travel weight and wilderness impact.

Our car-pool coordinators, Herman and Rich, are doing a fine job of arranging transportation; you'll be getting final travel information from them. Joel is likewise cooperating in a fine way to make the outing work well.

*One thing that has been going forward also is arrangements
for cooperative eating. Groups of twos or threes are getting together
and buying and planning to carry it communally. I encourage this;
it should result in more companionability and less luggage.*

*I expect to bring a community water supply from my 210-foot
deep well in Caswell County, approximately 20 gallons.
Please feel free to call on it for filling canteens, washing and cooking.
I am still planning to bring a portable jean/jeannette.
I believe we're well on the way to being organized. I hope not overly so.*

At Rich's apartment in Durham, we load two canoes atop Rich's van and four human beings and their gear inside. Rich has made room for gear by taking out some seats; thus the floor of the payload area is shared by persons and stuff. Annette, Bruce and I vie for the remaining passenger seat; and missing out, sit or recline on the floor. Rich does all the driving. At the motel in Folkston, Annette suggests that we can save money by placing box springs from both double beds on the floor, making four beds from two.

On Saturday morning we reach the put-in at Kingfisher Landing not long after an early breakfast. Eric and Jack have camped here all night. Some of us arrange gear in boats while all the drivers take vehicles to Stephen Foster Park and then are shuttled back to Kingfisher in Rich's van.

❖

Even after a lapse of nearly a decade, Kingfisher Landing feels comfortably familiar, with just a hint, as one looks across the broad canal, of the isolation we'll feel as the vegetation becomes thicker and more uniquely swamplike, the water trail narrower and more "closed-in." But as trip leader, I am giving minimum attention to such matters, focusing instead on circulating and giving hints about dressing boats and securing gear.

There are enough "old experienced" river canoeists in the group to minimize hysteria over the delay while we wait for the setters of the shuttle. Some of those waiting at the landing are antsy and frustrated, trying hard to keep their heels cool. Some non-driving paddling partners use their time making the boats swampworthy. This wait also provides all of us a chance to get acquainted with the old friends we haven't met yet. Anyone with whom one travels by water quickly becomes an "old friend."

After Rich and the other drivers return and before we launch the boats,

I receive a nice surprise. Joel gathers the group, walks over to me, gives a little speech of appreciation for my efforts in organizing the trip and presents me with the most beautiful wooden paddle I ever expect to own. I call it my "ceremonial" paddle. It's great for swamp canoeing; I wouldn't dream of using it in white water, where one violent encounter with a rock could be the death of it.

It is 11:00, not a bad starting time for Day One. We launch our parade of sixteen persons in eight canoes on the first broad mile of canal. Immediately I am struck anew with the wonder of all that sky reflected in the dark water.

The route will be the same as the one I have followed before. The terrain will be as described in **Trip Six - Afloat.** The experience, though, will necessarily be different in view of the greater numbers and lesser degree of closeness among the personnel. I can't describe each boater's experience of pulling the boat along first the broad canal and then, after a mile, a "track" of water barely wider than the beam of the boat. We travel through wetlands, prairie, forest and ponds. Some of us, surely, are having a novel and unique experience. Since I can't look inside the head, heart and gut of each tripper, let's take a look at the outsides.

I paddle at the head with Annette, with whom I have paddled before in more demanding waters: whitewater rivers. I have seen her progress markedly in her paddle skill and power, and we have become a pretty good team. With little need to communicate in voiced words, we can stay silent and not frighten wildlife, allowing for a greater chance that those farther back in the line may enjoy the creatures too.

Second in the caravan come Eric and brother Jack, two young fellows with considerable experience at roughing it in the wild. They have the youth, strength and skill to paddle circles around the rest of us but of course are too well-mannered to try.

Third come Herman and Rich, our travel coordinators. Rich, a medical equipment researcher, is also our shuttle director and quasi-official photographer. I have hiked with him on other Club outings. When we arrive at Maul Hammock, he paddles out immediately to get a panoramic photograph of our encampment and stays out on the lake to do some fishing.

Fourth in line come Will and Vangie, an attractive couple with different last names who give the impression of having enjoyed similar adventures in the past.

Fifth come Ken and Lorraine, an attractive couple with the same last name, clearly thrilled to be included in this once-in-a-lifetime experience.

Sixth: Jane and her 15-year-old son John, who have been with me on two outings before, both of them canoe trips (Dan River, New River). John is intrepid and friendly, lots of fun. Jane has dreams of exploring the wilds of Alaska — if she can find the right male partner.

Seventh: Susanna and Bruce, she an inveterate leader of canoe outings who will sell all her canoe gear and put her resources into spelunking. Bruce is a brilliant electrical engineer who carries on each outing a different outdoor guide to master some new aspect of nature.

Last comes Joel, leaning back in the stern of his boat and lazily stroking the water with his bent-shaft paddle while Allison in the bow watches out for alligators and the odd Southern Blue Flag (*Iris virginica*). I have camped and paddled with Allison before and even platonically shared a tent with her at Hanging Rock. Joel's boat, the "sweep," is custodian of the porta-john. When anyone has need of it, the proper protocol is to drop back to last position, pick up the pot from Joel and stay at the end of the line until finished with it (all other eyes in the group aimed strictly forward). All of these rules are a mere formality; actually, no one will use the pot *en route*.

In this condition we arrive at Maul Hammock.

In planning for the trip I have made the assumption that some members of the party will develop a certain stiffness in the shoulders after a day of paddling. This kind of travel is different from river travel. On flat water one is never coasting; if one isn't pulling forward with the paddle, the boat stops — unless the wind is blowing. Going somewhere on flat water requires constant use of the shoulder and back muscles, with resulting stiffness, especially if one is inexperienced and relies more on the shoulder muscles than on the larger, stronger back and abdominal muscles.

All this is prelude to telling you of my decision to take along almond-scented massage oil, curtains for privacy and other necessary accouterments in order to open Sammy Oliver's Massage Parlor on the camping platform after each day's trip. As Sammy Oliver, the proprietor, I offer basically two kinds of massages: (1) your Sammy (or semi-) massage, focusing only on the tired neck, back and shoulder muscles; and (2) your more ambitious, thorough-going Oliver (All-over) massage, in which the entire body gets the treatment. I soon find that curtains for privacy are not necessary. Only a few clients are willing to admit they need a widdle wubbing-kindness, and only of the Sammy variety. When I spread out the towel on the hard, bare boards of the platform, John says, "Sure," takes off his shirt and assumes the position. After the women hear John groan with delight and relief, it is easier for a couple of them to avail themselves of the free service.

Supper is a gourmet affair, at least for those who sup with Susanna (tofu and veggies). When bed-time arrives, we are tired enough to lie still and listen to night sounds, content with whatever tent mates we end up with. Eric and

Jack sleep under only their ponchos and thus have more direct encounters with the raccoons than the rest of us.

On Day Two we see the odd alligator sunning on the bank. The old bulls do not move at our approach; the youngsters, more easily intimidated, are likely to appear in our photographs as a splash of swamp water. We see, more stationary on the bank, an occasional swamp iris (*Iris versicolor,* Family *Iridaceae*); overhead, riding the breeze or perching atop a dead tree, a red-shouldered or red-tailed hawk; or, with luck, a fishy shape barely visible in the dark water.

Annette is keeping a list of her bird sightings and coming up with a fair sampling of the Refuge's 225 species. Among her prizes she lists the kingfisher (*Megaceryle alcyon*); gray catbird (*Dumatella carolinensis*); swamp sparrow (*Melospiza georgiana*); northern cardinal (*Cardinalis cardinalis*); golden-crowned kinglet (*Regulus calendula*); yellow-rumped warbler (*Dendroica coronata*); red-bellied woodpecker (*Melanerpes carolinus*); common yellowthroat (*Geothylpus richas*); eastern kingbird (*Tyrannus tyrannus*); common bob-white (*Colinus virginianus*); rufous-sided towhee (*Pipilo erythrophthalmus*); great egret (*Casmerodias albus*); cattle egret (*Bubulcus ibis*); American black duck — really a patterned dark brown *Anas rubripes*); great blue heron (*Ardea herodias*); little blue heron (*Florida caerulia*); northern parula warbler (*Parula americana*); red-shouldered hawk (*Buteo lineatus*); red-tailed hawk (*Buteo jamaicensis*); turkey vulture (*Carthartes aura*); black vulture (*Choragyps atratus*); white ibis (*Eudocimus albus*); cormorant (*Phalacrocorax*); and anhinga, with the seemingly superfluous scientific name *Anhinga anhinga,* a somewhat snakier bird than the cormorant.

No avian *aficionado,* I am hardly aware of her list-keeping as I pour on the paddle-power and she wields the binoculars, mostly at stopping-places. We are not in a hurry. Our day's work is a ten-mile paddle, admittedly a bit hard on back and shoulders, but lending itself to a slow, lazy pace. Little do I suspect (little does any of us expect) that birds will provide the high point of our Okefenokee adventure.

The high point of the day comes after dark, when we have set up at Big Water Lake and enjoyed our evening meal. Tired though we be, we are, after all (most of us) confirmed city-folk, accustomed to an evening of entertainment. But since we are outdoor persons as well, we acknowledge that a True Life Adventure is better than a rented video. We climb back into canoes and glide as silently as we can along the narrow trail, trying to catch in the flashlight beam the frogs that are serenading us; then we stroke the boat across Big Water Lake, seeing pairs of red eyes which we know belong to alligators floating with only their eyes above the surface and droning out their baritone continuo.

After all this activity and before bed-time, two super-cleanly members of our group, including my usually-sedate paddling partner, feel so grubby that they risk a dip in the 'gator-infested water of Big Water Lake. I do not witness this event but hear about it next morning.

"I hope you didn't use soap; that would be against Refuge rules."

On the morning of Day 3 we break fast, wash up, pack and prepare to depart.

Now comes (for me) the high point of the trip. Against the background of frog, bird and insect sounds, we become aware of a new sound that grows rapidly louder, and suddenly the croaking of at least two dozen sandhill cranes (*Grus canadensis*) passes directly over the camping platform. We drop what's in our hands and stand gawking at the pale bustled gray giants with the red scarlet crowns. Squawking their way northward on wings wider than I am tall, the cranes remind me of a chorus of rickety antique escalators.

Our voices now hushed by the awareness of our undeserved good fortune, through the dark cypress alleys we file, stroking silently past lounging alligators on slippery logs, under ghostly festoons of Spanish moss. All too soon we arrive at the busy traffic in the broad Suwannee. And all too soon we turn left and head down the long, narrow canal to the take-out at Stephen Foster Park. Swamp images dance in our brains all night.

We emerge from the Refuge in separate vehicles on Easter Sunday morning. Our little party of four pauses at the gate for a souvenir photograph. For a few miles of I-95 Annette and I entertain our companions with old Easter hymns recalled from Sunday School.

The clearest memory that we carry back into our busy lives is the sight and sound of Sandhill cranes red-headed, gray-bodied, their voices rickety and mechanical. ❖

THIRTEEN - AFLOAT
BITTERSWEET MISTLETOE REPORT

—THIRTEEN - AFLOAT—

Bittersweet Mistletoe Report

ADVENTURE SITE
*The Upper Little River, Harnett County
Lumbee River, Scotland County
North Carolina*

There's more than one way to achieve immortality. Grasping, initiating or perpetuating a tradition is a pretty good one. That's what I thought I was doing in founding the Annual Sprig Outing (for background see **Trips Three - Afloat** and **Four - Afloat**). Sadly, the tradition has proved thin and fragile; it appears to be at serious risk of demise.

The origins of tradition tend to become lost in the mists of antiquity; thus there's a lot I can't remember about the early years of the Sprig Outing. One reliable date is December of 1983, the time of the First Annual. I can't honestly remember whether the trip narrated in **Four - Afloat** was the First or Second Annual. In the following pages I intend to narrate the Tenth Annual and refer in various ways to other trips. Before I get into any of that, I must wind the spring by speaking of MISTLETOE.

Many of us have heard the name of the famous anthropologist Sir James George Frazer (1854-1941) and seen references to the title of his best-known work, *The Golden Bough* (1891). Fewer may be aware that the golden bough celebrated in his title refers to the European parasitic shrub mistletoe (*Viscum album*), which has somehow bequeathed its name to several (presumably similar) American parasites, such as *Phoradendron flavescens*. Perhaps even fewer may be aware of why mistletoe came to be called the "golden bough."

It doesn't seem logical, does it, to call mistletoe "golden" when those of us who have ever seen it at all know it to be an "evergreen," like pine and cedar. But if you hang pine or cedar to brighten your holidays with green, and you forget to take it down, will it stay green? Not likely.

But why would you leave your mistletoe up long enough for it to turn into a golden bough? To find the answer, you'll have to study mistletoe's history in some such source as Sir James Frazer's famous work. Reading it, you'll learn that "at York, in the eighteenth century, mistletoe was carried to the high altar of the Cathedral and a public amnesty and 'universal liberty' was proclaimed . . . . The traditional privilege of kissing any woman found under mistletoe is a relic of the same thing."[1] Hung over the door lintel, it was a sign that one had forgiven one's enemies. When I read about that application of the mistletoe, I said "Aha! Here's an opportunity for spiritual growth"; and from then on each year's mistletoe stayed above my front door from one winter solstice to the next, growing plenty golden in the process. Both leaves and stem acquired that golden hue, a lovely symbol of the psychological and moral value of keeping the spirit free of the burden of hate.

Mistletoe, James Frazer informs us, "from time immemorial has been an object of superstitious veneration in Europe,"[2] and he gives many examples, amazingly varied, of the functions of this remarkable shrub in the lives of our forbears (see Appendix, "**The Mythology of Mistletoe**").

Mistletoe-garnering has been a worthy project both as a fund-raiser and as a preserver of a cultural tradition. It's fun, and it's at least as good an excuse as fishing or golf for getting out into the natural world. Luckily, I am not the only one who has thought so. The Headwaters Group has held an annual Sprig Outing each December since 1983.

In 1992, a goodly number of persons, representing the Sierra Club and the Dan River Trail Association, respond to the invitation. On a December Saturday we gather in the parking lot of Hardee's in Lillington. Then fourteen persons, in six canoes, put in on the swollen Lower Little River (tributary of the Cape Fear), where the river is crossed by NC Highway 210.

Thad, co-coordinator of the trip, paddles with Simon, our stalwart champion grappler. Son Reed and his wife Elizabeth paddle my second-best *Mohawk*. My old river pal Sue and her friend Norman team up in Sue's yellow *Blue Hole* boat. Joe and Dorothy carry with them as passenger daughter Jennifer. Pete, sole representative of the Sierra Club's Capital Group, paddles with his children Chrissie and John. Lea and I are in *Red Mohawk*. A larger group would be hard to manage. This group is just big enough — and intimate enough — to comprise a good working team. Each participant is personally acquainted with at least one of the co-coordinators. Two bring with them long-handled pruning loppers. I have my painter's pole, extensible to 20 feet; and Simon and Thad have brought a very long tree branch. We are ready to garner mistletoe.

As for cooperation, no Sprig Outing goes better. The lead boaters are spotters (for most of the trip, this is Lea and I). Lea in the bow scans the tree canopy for promising sprigs, those not too high up in trees overhanging the river and preferably sporting lots of branches with fat gray berries. I in the stern control the boat and reconnoiter for accessibility: is the sprig so situated that it can be captured by us fourteen boaters maneuvering our six boats to best advantage?

If prospects continue good, Lea and I eddy up by turning and paddling upstream until she, in the bow, can grasp something stable, preferably a tree on the bank. Then the others, holding to our boat or to something more stable, try to broaden the target area for falling sprigs, positioning at least one boat so that the pole wielder will have clear access to the mistletoe. This is not so easy as it may sound; often intervening branches of the tree get in the way; and then that particular sprig must be abandoned.

"Oh, well, let it stay and provide spoors for next year's crop."

Sometimes the sprig becomes snagged as it falls.

Poles often change hands, passed from boat to boat, depending on who has the clearest shot and how tired the grappler has become in wielding the heavy pole. Simon is the champion, both in skill and staying power.

This is the fun part of the trip: all six boats athwart (or in a string from the upstream tree through boats and painters to the wielder right under the tempting cluster), all of us with a common aim: to bring 'em back still full of luscious berries. Many "ooh's" and "ah's" go up in chorus as a specimen particularly endowed with branches and berries comes tumbling down. Sprigs caught in low branches are often loosened by someone's paddle as pole wielders continue to grope and slash higher up.

"Look out, John; here it comes — right on your head!"

Or: "Grab it, Sue! It's floating toward you!" (It doesn't float long; it's heavier than water and, alas, often sinks before anyone can stop it.)

No wonder Thad says, during and after the trip, "It's too much fun not to continue this tradition."

Lunch on the bank is an occasion for swapping tales of Sprig Outings past, comparing sales strategies and expressing determination to continue this annual event.

Shortly after lunch I am guilty of poor judgment and rash action, perhaps also of *hubris* based on today's fine spirit of cooperation. The sprig is quite low and near the bank — easily within reach of any of the poles and maybe even of a person carefully standing in a boat and reaching up. The river at this point is narrow and swift, the branch a foot above my head as I kneel in the boat.

"Grab the branch!" I call to Lea in the bow. This is a mistake, as the boat is pointed downstream; the bow paddler must not grab a branch in these circumstances. In any case, Lea tries but succeeds only in turning the boat broadside to the current. Then I grab for the branch and succeed in flipping both of us into the frigid river.

I spare you the details of the "rescue," of the solicitous offers by Sue and Norman and the well-meant advice by nearly all of the others. Pete knows just how to empty the boat even though the bank is steep and muddy and the maneuver must be carried out without using the bank. I have learned this maneuver from Howard Leuhrs during the Fifth or Sixth Annual Sprig Outing: how to invert one boat across another to empty the water; and have subsequently used it to help a couple of fishermen on the New River. Now I am too cold and too upset to manage the operation. Thank goodness for Veteran canoer Pete, who takes over while Lea and I stand shivering on the bank. My main desire, aside from salvaging the mistletoe tied into and now floating in the water-filled boat, is to get back into action pronto paddling downriver to stave off hypothermia. I've been in the water a bit too long but am prepared to continue wet, knowing dry clothes await me at the take-out.

Thad and I agree that Lea and I will continue to run "Point" and that the rest of the group will pick up the pace. It is approaching four o'clock and sunset; it will soon be too dark — and too cold — for safety and comfort on the river.

"Well," observes Lea philosophically, when between rapid strokes I keep apologizing as we speed down the river, "if anyone had to go in, we were as well prepared as anyone else." She means both sartorially (clad in polypropylene, Thermax™ and wool) and emotionally: we've swum before and survived, and we know that an involuntary swim, even in frigid water, doesn't spell the end of the world.

"And another good thing," I add, "it's early enough that we can see and enjoy this section. Other years it's been dusk as we've traveled through here."

We take out at 4:30, late enough this close to the solstice. Cooperatively we haul the boats up the steep and slippery concrete bridge support to the road.

❖

For the first five years, I was the one who led the outings, heroically assisted in at least one of these years by Dave Knowles (see **Trip Four - Afloat**). Howard Leuhrs and Tommy Cocke came aboard in 1988 as participants, and Howard led the outing for a couple of years before leaving the area. His departure put me back at the helm in 1992. By 1993 Thad and Simon had become the chief honchos. Thad led in 1994 and co-led with me in 1995. Solstice time in 1996 would have been the Fourteenth Annual. But in December of 1996 Simon was the father of twin newborns, and Thad had business obligations that kept him off the river. Key members of the Trail Association were likewise preoccupied.

Will the golden bough break? Will the ribbon of Sprig Outings rip?

With anticipation of the joy of a family gathering but a twinge of sadness for the Sprig Outing, I drive to Laurinburg for a holiday visit. My son-in-law Scott, bless his heart, not only knows my attachment to the mistletoeing tradition; he is also familiar with many places where the roads of Scotland County cross the Lumbee River and its tributary creeks. We canvass these in his '69 pick-up, in company with granddaughter Valerie (age almost three) and River Dog Rusty (age 16). We take a ladder, "just in case," but though we see some rich bouquets of the famous parasite, some low enough to reach by ladder, all are growing in trees that have their feet in the water; no way can we place the ladder to gain access.

Then, serendipity!

Next day, we haul out all the bicycles for a family ride on the campus of the local college. The campus is deserted; the students have left for the Christmas holiday. In part we are indulging granddaughter Brooke, age 6, who has just learned to balance her two-wheeler and glories in her new skill. "She's like a 16-year-old who's just got a driver's license," says her mother; "she rides everywhere." In part, also, we are out for family togetherness: Granddad, daughter Lydian, son-in-law Scott, eager Brooke and intrepid little Valerie, with training wheels on her seemingly too-large-for-her-littleness two-wheeler. We certainly do not expect to find mistletoe.

But behold ! as we ride past a low live-oak tree on the deserted campus: mistletoe! Scott drives home for his lopper.

The lopper won't reach high enough, but Granddad is determined, and he hasn't forgotten how to climb a li'l ol' live-oak tree and toss down some lovely sprigs.

And so, daughter Lydian's house, already beautifully decorated with natural greenery, acquires the added grace of mistletoe in the den and on the outdoor lamps mounted over the garage; and during my 1996 Christmas trip north to visit siblings, I can do as last year: brighten the holidays for the service station attendant, the waitress, the Welcome Center host and the convenience store clerk, with gifts of mistletoe. Not to mention brightening the chandeliers of my Pittsburgh niece, nephew and siblings.

As Winter Solstice 1997 approaches, the "usual suspects" to lead a group mistletoeing in Little River swamp are less inclined than ever. The demise of Durham's one canoe outfitter makes the participation of the Headwaters Group less feasible; and dousings in December waters have dampened the spirits in both that group and the Trail Association. For the second consecutive year I content myself with a family bicycle ride to the little live-oak tree in Laurinburg, where we can still find some very nice branches of *Phoradendron flavescens*.

Fast forward to late summer of 1998. For some inexplicable reason perhaps related to the generic inflexibility of us septuagenarians, I still harbor thoughts of reviving the Sprig Outing. I call my old friend Annette, with whom I have paddled before (see **Trip Twelve - Afloat**). She is now a Sierra Club outings chair.

"I'll announce it in the Triangle area newsletters," Annette promises (actually, it seems to go out to all groups in the state). And since she is the official liaison for the Sierra Club, she feels obliged to scout the river with me beforehand.

It has been a dry summer, the kind that keeps even hard-core river runners off the rivers. They know they'll do less floating than hauling over rocks and dry sand bars. Nevertheless, on November 21, four of us launch two tandem boats at the bridge where NC Highway 210 crosses the Upper Little River.

For this scouting trip, I have recruited a tandem partner known to be a strong and capable paddler: son Reed. Annette has found Melissa, an artist from Raleigh.

"We'll be off the river by 4:00," I assure Reed and Annette, each of whom has an evening engagement. We are all aware that the sun at 4:00 will be low in the sky and that the cold will set in quickly. Aware of the chance of a spill with resulting hypothermia, I have left my sleeping bag in the cap of the truck.

Scouting from the bridge, we can see clearly that to launch here will be out of the question: too many rocks, too little water. Downstream, river left, is a frequently-used launching place, where the water is deeper and less rocky. Reed reluctantly accepts a post in the bow while I mount the stern of *Red Mohawk*. Melissa in the bow and Annette in the stern launch my old green *Mohawk*, which I have borrowed back from river pal Trent. We set shuttle and launch.

All goes well — for a few minutes. Then we come to rapids which would be great fun with water to float us over them. Today, though, we use our paddles as poles to push off rocks covered by only an inch of water, when we need three inches minimum. I am out of the boat, wading and pulling on the painter before we have been on the river ten minutes, grateful for the neoprene socks under my neoprene boots. Leaving Reed in charge of the boat, I wade upstream, where the women, riding the green *Mohawk*, are well stuck.

"I'm going to get out and pull," Melissa says.

"Wait a minute," I request. "You don't want to wet those tennis shoes."
I call to Reed. "Dig in the red dry-bag and haul out my second-best river boots." Sad to say, broken glass is everywhere, even in river beds.

Melissa, accustomed for nine years to wading barefoot on coarse Hawai'ian coral, soon becomes impatient with boots and wades in her bare feet.

We struggle through three football fields' worth of dry rapids while just downstream, river left, three old codgers stand on the bank watching our strivings with some amusement. While waiting for the women to cope with the last of the shallows, Reed and I look around and see signs of an effort to clear the river of down trees from the recent hurricane: cut ends of big limbs sticking out from the bank. We paddle over to the three spectators.

"You can paddle for about another mile," they say. What they imply is that after a mile, we'll find the river blocked by down trees.

We float. We stop and grapple for mistletoe. Reed experiments with the carabiner arrangement for tying to a tree on the bank. Annette and Melissa come athwart to enlarge the target area for falling sprigs. We take turns wielding the painter's pole and bring down some lovely specimens. Between stops, Melissa digs her paddle in the super-energetic Hawai'ian "outrigger" style. Reed is both amused at her style and impressed with her power.

That goes on until lunch time on the bank, between a cleared field and a narrow buffer of rare river cane. Discussion ranges from Melissa's Hawai'i years to Reed's Liberia sojourn in the Peace Corps to Annette's misgivings about the Sprig Outing, announced for the first Saturday in December. Clearly, as she sees it, an unfledged group will not be able to cope with the low-water challenges we are encountering.

Reluctantly, I agree. "I don't suppose it would be worthwhile to scout the Lower Little. It'll be worse than the Upper."

"Anyway," Annette concludes, "no one but Melissa has called me."

"Lucky we hard-core paddlers were available to find out what's here," Reed observes.

On the river again, we soon find that the evidence of clearing alternates with evidence of incomplete clearing. There <u>are</u> fresh white butt-ends on the banks, aimed at us, but there are also down trees in the river. Some block only part of the river's width, making it possible to skirt around or slip under. Others block the entire river; then we have a choice: lift over or portage. I've had plenty of experience at the former and am not intimidated. In this lazy current, it's fairly easy to slide the boat alongside, slip from boat to log, wait for Reed to do the same, kick the stern upstream, lift the bow up and over, tugging until the stern splashes into the water downriver (careful to keep a good hold on the stern painter), bring boat alongside again, hold while Reed mounts, mount while Reed holds and shove off.

One trick I have learned is that the boat, while being tugged out of the water, across the log or back afloat again, is heavy enough and stable enough to help the boaters balance on the log while tugging. It will take Melissa and Annette a while to refine their technique to this point.

Once they have seen us perform this maneuver, Annette and Melissa undertake it as my son and I coach. Unfortunately, the first time they try, Annette slips off the log and goes waist-deep into the cold river. She doesn't seem to be in a hurry to get back on the log. Melissa is on the log river right holding the bow; Annette is in the river left holding the stern.

"Get out of the water, Annette !" I shout as Reed and I paddle back to help.

"Oh, well, while I'm here I may as well help get the boat over the log."

"Get out of the water, Annette," I shout with increased volume and urgency. Hasn't she heard of hypothermia? Doesn't she know that the sooner she gets out, the less body heat she'll lose?

After three or four more urgings, she climbs out to continue the transfer of the boat across the down tree. There's no point in Reed's and my trying to help with that; we'd only be in the way. A down tree, especially one without substantial girth, makes but a slender, slippery platform for a working party.

As we continue downstream, and as the sun declines toward the cool end of the day, we perform this maneuver a dozen times, fifteen times, twenty times (Reed claims he counted twenty-five), continually hoping that we'll soon see the last of these strainers but being repeatedly disappointed.

"Uh-oh! Look downstream."

"Ay! Another one."

Four o'clock comes, and though we are now in the most meandering part of the section, which I know is close to the bridge, our progress continues to be slow. Every hundred yards or so, and sometimes more often, we come to another strainer. My noble son sheds his Gore-Tex® pants and passes them to Annette, who is in need of a windbreaker from waist downward.

Since Reed and I have paddled together before, we have got most of the maneuvers down to a science. The women, less accustomed to one another's styles and less of a team, are not keeping up, and we don't want to leave them.

"What do you think, Reed? Shall we switch partners? It's after 4:00, and it's starting to get cold. Is there some diplomatic way we can suggest it without offending a pair of feminists?"

"How about asking if anyone's tired?"

"Good idea."

We beach and wait for the green boat, and after considerable discussion, Melissa climbs into the bow of the red boat while I assume the stern of the green.

We are not home free yet. We are getting tired and irritable, and around each bend we are greeted by another down tree. Melissa and Reed are apparently profiting from both Melissa's powerful "outrigger" stroke and Reed's strength in boat-lifting. Soon they are out of sight. For my part, I find my partner willing to discuss the fine details of each little piece of the process even while I am in waist-deep water hefting my end. At two strainers we try with some success using speed to get up onto and a rocking motion to get over a log an inch below the surface. At another we are able, by ducking down in turn, to float under a tree's "low bridge." At still another, the "bridge" is low enough to knock off my ten-gallon hat. And then there's the one which, after Annette has passed under and the boat is halfway through, I find is easier to step over than duck under. I was never so glad to hear traffic and glimpse the U.S. 401 bridge through the trees.

It has not been a good trip, and I can't in good conscience invite anyone else to try it. But I'm too stubborn to give up. On Sunday, November 29, on the way home from Thanksgiving with the Laurinburg branch of the family, I do some reconnoitering on the shuttle road, after which, armed with a telephone number, I get permission to launch. The site is one I recognize from the scouting trip, ideal because situated between the upstream dry rapids and the downstream 25 channel-blocking trees. All systems are "GO."

And so on December 5 the Sprig Outing proceeds, with a slightly revised plan and six paddlers in three boats. It's been a long time since I've both put in and taken out at the same place for a river trip — never before on the Sprig Outing. We have a sedate trip, and each person brings home a richness of mistletoe and even some holly.

The Sprig Season is not over yet. While paddling with new friends in the Lumber River Canoe Club on the Saturday after Thanksgiving, I rashly agreed to lead a "Sprig" trip December 12. I invite Ray Fidler, a member of the canoe class I taught at daughter Lydian's church, and we soon become a good team for both paddling and grappling. Charles and Marsha must have enjoyed last Saturday on the Upper Little, for they join us again today on the Lumbee. Canoe Club president Marshall Thompson and his wife Charlotte and longtime river pals Elizabeth and Mike Britt and their tiny dog Blackie show up, along with a dozen other eager paddlers. This is too many to form one group free of traffic jams on this "Class C" (relatively swift), winding blackwater river; the group gets strung out and roughly divided between those interested in mistletoeing and those along for the pure joy of river travel. It is one more fine day on the river.

It has been a busy late November and early December, a satisfying prelude to the Solstice / Chanukah / Christmas holiday time. I have experienced a good mix of river companions from two Sierra and three canoe club groups.

Before I left Durham to move to the country, I mentioned the Sprig Outing to my neighbor Ed, a columnist for the *Herald-Sun*. He seemed alarmed.

"Mistletoe — isn't that an endangered species?"

No, Ed; but mistletoeing in the swamp is an endangered tradition.

The February 1999 newsletter of the Lumber River Canoe Club carries this report of the December trip: "Forrest Altman did the scouting and arranged a 'Sprig Outing' for those who had the mistletoe mania. It was a successful trip with plenty of water and boaters in 10 boats. *A tradition has been revived* [Italics mine]."

I hope so. But the question remains: Will anyone take up the leadership of the Annual Sprig Outing? ❖

---

[1] *The New Golden Bough*, Abridged from Sir James Frazer's classic work by Theodor H. Gaster (New York: New American Library, 1964), p. 749.

[2] Ibid., p. 674.

ON MISTLETOE

Selections from *The New Golden Bough*

Abridged from Sir James Frazer's Classic work by Theodor H. Gaster (New York: New American Library, 1964)

Page

674 "From time immemorial the mistletoe has been an object of superstitious veneration in Europe."

673 Mistletoe struck and killed the Norse god Balder, whose life was between heaven and earth.

679 Balder was identified with the oak, and mistletoe was regarded as "the seat of life of the oak"; so long as the mistletoe is intact nothing can happen to the oak. "The conception of the mistletoe as the seat of life in the oak would naturally be suggested [to] primitive people by the observation that while the oak is deciduous, the mistletoe which grows on it is evergreen. In winter the sight of its fresh foliage among the bare branches must have been hailed by worshippers as a sign that the divine life had ceased to animate the branches yet survived in the mistletoe, as the heart of a sleeper beats when his body is motionless."

690 "The mistletoe owes its mystic character to its not growing on the ground."

691 A popular superstition held that "at certain times the mistletoe blazed out into a supernatural golden glow."

692 "Breton peasants hung up great bunches of mistletoe in front of their cottages, and in the month of June these bunches were conspicuous for the bright golden tinge of their foliage."

183 "In Herefordshire, England, the 'bush,' i. e., the hawthorn or black thorn bush, which, with the mistletoe bough, had been hung in the farmhouse kitchen since the last year, was ceremonially burned on January 1. During the operation, a new one was made. It was believed that without this ceremony, there would be no crops."

692 "Mistletoe is gathered either at midsummer or Christmas — that is, at the summer or winter solstice — and it is supposed to possess the power of revealing treasures in the earth." Thus in Sweden it is used in divining rods.

692 "In Sweden mistletoe is still kept in houses as a safeguard against conflagration."

674 Gathered without its touching the ground, it was a particularly powerful medicine.

675 The Druids cut mistletoe with a golden sickle; to cut it with iron would destroy its efficacy.

674 A mistletoe called *tob* is venerated in Senegambia, West Africa.

676 In the Swiss Tyrol, mistletoe is believed to be able "under certain conditions" (unspecified) to open all locks.

676 In Austria, "a twig of mistletoe . . . laid on the threshold" is thought to prevent nightmares.

676 In the north of England you can cause your dairy herd to succeed if you give a touch of mistletoe to the first cow that calves after New Year's Day.

676 In Sweden mistletoe is efficacious against mischievous trolls.

749 "At York, in the eighteenth century, mistletoe was carried to the high altar of the Cathedral and a public amnesty and 'universal liberty' was proclaimed . . . The traditional privilege of kissing any woman found under mistletoe is a relic of the same thing."

761 Mistletoe has been found on: apple, black poplar, horse chestnut, maple, sallow, locust, larch, Scottish fir, acacia, laburnum, pear, large-leaved sallow, spruce, service *(pyrus domestica)*, olive, walnut, plum, common laurel, medlar, grey poplar, hazel, ash, lime, rowan, crab, white thorn, silver fir and pine fir.

GLOSSARY

beach (verb transitive, verb intransitive) haul or run ashore.

beam breadth of a boat at its widest place.

bilge the bottom of the inside of the boat; i.e., the part that floods when water comes over the gunwales.

cairn a heap of stones piled up as a landmark.

bow the forward part of the boat.

carabiner "an oblong metal ring with a spring clip, used in mountaineering to attach a running rope to a piton or similar device" (American Heritage Dictionary).

channel a passage through which a boat can pass.

climax forest forest in which hardwoods have reached their fullest maturity and diversity.

current flow of water, with the effect of providing motion downstream but complicating navigation.

draw stroke a stroke aimed at moving the boat (or one's portion of it) toward the side on which the person is paddling. The person reaches out as far as feasible and "pulls" the water toward the boat.

draft the depth to which a boat sinks when placed in the water.

dress arrange a boat's load for best balance and greatest ease of movement through the water.

D-ring ring shaped like the letter "D" anchored to the deck and used for tying down a boat's freight.

dry-bag bag made of waterproof material used to keep items dry in case of rain, splash or submersion. Few dry bags are completely effective if submerged for long or under pressure from depth or strong current.

eddy up stop where the water downstream of an obstacle is flowing upstream while the surrounding water is rushing downstream in the current.

ferry cross the river.

gauge any item used to determine water depth and navigability.

G.O.R.P. "Good Old Raisins and Peanuts"; or any high-energy concoction of nearly any combination of dry finger-food, mostly nuts and seeds and, of course, raisins.

grunch pad skid plate, extra skin of Kevlar® or urethane applied as protection for bow or stern to absorb shock and wear.

❖ 26 WILDERNESS ADVENTURES: AFOOT & AFLOAT

gunwale the top rim around the boat.

hydraulic the force exerted by the momentum of water falling across the face of a dam or other vertical surface, a force which creates a tenacious and virtually irresistible rolling motion at the foot of the "fall," hard to escape from

keel ridge along the centerline under the hull of the boat, designed to help the craft travel in a straight line (and make it harder to turn).

kick-seine fine-mesh portable net about four feet square used to catch tiny fish or macroinvertevrates.

painter length of line attached to bow or stern, used mainly for securing boat to bank or dock.

pile artificial fabric whose thickness is designed to make it approximately as warm as wool, even when wet.

point lead boat in a river party.

polypropylene artificial fabric designed to be worn next to the skin. Body heat wicks moisture through it, away from the body, keeping the body dry and able to retain its heat.

poop flip end to end when following water overwhelms the stern.

pry push water away from the boat to move the boat, or one's portion of it, toward the side opposite the one on which one is paddling.

rapid a place in the river or stream where water falling over rocks or other surface increases in velocity.

rip a section of river or stream underlain by large stones relatively equal in size over which a sufficient body of water flows to create a turbulent but navigable surface.

river right the right side of the river as one faces downstream. It's still river right when one is facing upstream.

rudder (noun, verb) stroke executed to slow or turn the boat.

saddle earth form from which the terrain rises in opposing directions and drops in the opposing directions at a 90° angle to the rising ground.

skid plate see grunch pad.

slack water calm water without current or turbulence.

standing wave wave that does not change its position, usually caused by an underwater rock or other stationary object.

stern the rear portion of the boat.

strainer any obstruction which hampers or prevents downstream progress of boat or boater but not water; e.g., a branch reaching out from the bank; a tree down across the channel or tightly-spaced rocks.

swamp (verb) fill with water, making the craft difficult or impossible to maneuver

sweep stroke executed in the stern which, starting far forward and close to the boat, draws a backwards "C" on the water and has the effect of turning the boat toward the opposite side from the one on which the boater is paddling.

tandem with a partner.

thwart structural brace reaching across the boat from gunwale to gunwale to help the craft retain its shape or support a seat.

tongue the triangularly shaped area of water downstream from an obstruction, which a skillful boater looks for in "reading" the river for the best, least obstructed channel.

trough the elongated "valley" between waves, hazardous to any craft caught in it parallel to its boundaries; the rocking of the boat in a trough makes it difficult to prevent water from coming in over the gunwales.

turbidity the suspended matter in the water, rendering it murky or dark in color.

turbulence disturbance of the water, choppiness which threatens to pour over the gunwales

upstream ferry river crossing with bow pointed roughly upstream at a slight angle to the current so that the current moves the boat across the stream while the paddlers' strokes keep it from slipping prematurely downstream.

wake (noun) the visible track of turbulence left by something moving through the water.

wet exit an escape into the water, usually said of a kayaker, from a craft no longer under control.

ACKNOWLEDGMENTS

I am grateful to Marguerite Clark for her editorial wisdom, acuity and compassion.

Thanks to Doug Shumate and Gene Stanfield for their critical reading of an early draft.

Thanks to the New American Library for permission to quote passages of *The New Golden Bough,* Abridged by Theodor H. Gaster (1964).

Thanks for the maps, John. For the lovely design, Renée. Thanks, Trent, for all the picture-taking. Thanks, Elizabeth, for the hours of "playing" with the cover.

And thanks, family, for your help with decision-making (Scott, Diana, Elizabeth, Lydian, Reed, Grace, Betty, Marilyn and Jim).

I am immensely grateful to those dedicated outdoor leaders who presided over my wilderness novitiate; and to all of the companions who have ventured with me into the Great Outdoors.

AFTERWORD

YOU FORTUNATE AMERICANS: A BRITISH PERSPECTIVE

Following is an excerpt from a letter written to the author, after a first reading of the manuscript of "26 Wilderness Adventures."

My response [to your book] is much as it was over the *Dan River Book* — insights into the life of the author (and friend) which otherwise would have been lost to me and the strangeness of it all to one brought up in a country lacking a "wilderness." Of course we have our "outdoor folk": campers, hill walkers, climbers, pot-holers,* divers, canoeists, sailors, fishermen, and so on — but we do not have the great tracts of forest, mountain, desert, river and stream for them to explore — the lungs of your great country. To read *26 Wilderness Adventures* is to escape the cities, the malls, the freeways, the noise and bustle for a while to inhabit a more ancient world of forests, rivers, trails and the creatures for whom it is home.

Dennis Chorley
Retired university teacher
Birmingham University

August 25, 1999
Forge House
Clunbury
Shropshire

* spelunkers